SCIENCE
IN THE CITY

SERIES | RACE AND EDUCATION

Series edited by H. Richard Milner IV

SCIENCE
IN THE CITY

CITY

CULTURALLY RELEVANT
STEM EDUCATION

BRYAN A. BROWN

HARVARD EDUCATION PRESS
CAMBRIDGE, MASSACHUSETTS

Third Printing, 2021

Paperback ISBN 978-1-68253-374-1
Library Edition ISBN 978-1-68253-375-8

Library of Congress Cataloging-in-Publication data is on file.

Published by Harvard Education Press,
an imprint of the Harvard Education Publishing Group

Harvard Education Press
8 Story Street
Cambridge, MA 02138

Cover Design: Ciano Design
Cover Photo: JGI/Tom Grill/Getty Images
The typefaces used in this book are Agenda, Helvetica Neue, Latienne, and Lulo Clean.

This book is dedicated to the bright shining stars that I fly closest to each day. Cameron, Simone, and Cheryl, I pray each day gives you more joy and that your joy impacts the world.

CONTENTS

SERIES FOREWORD

by H. Richard Milner IV
Race and Education Series Editor

BRYAN A. BROWN'S *Science in the City: Culturally Relevant STEM Education* provocatively expands the Race and Education Series. In it, Brown uses story to advance empirical evidence about what it means to learn and teach science—particularly in large metropolitan environments. Drawing from rich, life-altering moments he has experienced as a learner, teacher, and advocate and researcher of science and STEM, he shepherds readers through a complex maze of race, STEM, people, learning, and teaching. In his words, "We were selling a vision of [STEM] educational success that did not make sense for many kids. Teachers were teaching science, but they forgot that we are not teaching *science*; instead, we are teaching *people*. We want the people to learn science, but ultimately, we are teaching people and we cannot act as if they do not matter."

Brown makes it abundantly clear that science and more broadly STEM are cultural spaces that should be available to everyone, regardless of geography or zip code, race or ethnicity, socioeconomic status, or sexual orientation. And this book is written for everyone who endeavors to know more about the ethos of STEM: parents and families; community members; and district personnel such as superintendents, teachers, coaches, school counselors, social workers, psychologists and psychiatrists. As Brown describes it, "The show *The Big*

Bang Theory is broadcast to millions each week and sends a resounding message about who belongs in science. The stereotypes about who can become a scientist do not merely exist in television, they are tropes that have been reinforced for generations. These stereotypes indirectly reference a perception of who should *not* be a scientist. If white, awkward men are scientists, then are cool Latinx women immediately out of the consideration? Stereotypes work this way. They frame an expectation and establish a seed of doubt for those who dare to defy the stereotype." An accessibly written text, a call to rethink a field, an invitation to question what we believe we know about teaching and learning, and challenge to teach STEM in ways that honor, acknowledge, and draw from the many strengths of the students who tend to be placed on the margins of STEM—especially black and brown students—every practicing and preservice teacher of STEM should read this book. Like other storytelling, data-driven, life-changing texts such as Derrick Bell's *Faces at the Bottom of the Well*, Lisa Delpit's *Other People's Children*, and Ron Suskind's *A Hope in the Unseen*, this book is a must-read for any of us in the struggle for racial justice, equity, and liberty.

A central goal of the Race and Education series is to advance a critical, forward-thinking body of research on race that contributes to policy, theory, practice, and action. Although the series will advance scholarship in race studies, a central objective is to assist educators—real teachers, school counselors, administrators, coaches, and outside-of-school providers—in their efforts to center the very humanity of students whose needs are far from being understood, responded to, and met in schools and in society.

Several interrelated objectives guide the series:

- to study race and develop explicit recommendations for eliminating racism, discrimination, and other forms of oppression from educational efforts and institutions

- to address race by means of multidisciplinary expertise and approaches
- to examine various layers of inequity through micro-, meso-, and macrolevel lenses that will expose individual and systemic barriers that prevent equitable opportunities for students of color
- to explore the many assets and strengths of students, communities, and families, thereby challenging inaccurate narratives, policies, and practices which suggest that students of color need "fixing," and instead reinforcing how students of color succeed when mechanisms are in place to support them
- to advance scholarly attention to aspects of racism and discrimination while also (and most importantly) offering real, action-driven assistance to educators and others who work with and on behalf of students of color inside and outside of schools as institutions

Grounded in and substantiated by empirical research, the series aims to highlight action designed to help solve problems of race in education. In this sense, it will look to address both societal issues and educational practices. The books included in the series will be developed to highlight scholarship from leading researchers in the field as well as emerging scholars and will investigate mechanisms, systems, structures and practices that have a real bearing on students' opportunities to learn.

Racial justice is arguably the most important educational imperative of our time. Considering the inextricable links between society and education, educators have the potential to help equip students with knowledge, tools, attitudes, dispositions, mind-sets, beliefs, and practices to create a world that is truly equitable for its citizenry. Series titles will attend to issues both inside and outside of schools, shedding light on what matters and how we, in education, can improve practices that systemically improve the life chances of students.

Above all, the Race and Education series asks the important question, *Do we have the fortitude to center race in our work, or will we continue going about our business, our work, as usual?* I am always mindful of curriculum theorist Beverly Gordon's provocative observation that "critiquing your own assumptions about the world—especially if you believe the world works for you"—is an arduous endeavor.[1] At the very heart of this series is an explicit challenge to those in power to work for the good of humanity, to interrupt systems, policies, and practices that work only for some while others remain underserved. It asks: How do the effects of poverty and compromised opportunities in transportation, housing, and employment manifest themselves in how communities respond to social (in)justice? What role does and should education play in understanding and responding to these manifestations? What roles do teachers play in helping students develop insights about the salience of race in society? How do education policy makers respond to these realities when making decisions about what gets covered in the curriculum? The books in this series will address many of these questions about race, racism, and discrimination to advance what we know in education and to move us toward a more equitable education system.

Indeed, a primary premise of the series is that we must learn from a diverse range of disciplines to build and sustain efforts on behalf of students who continue to be underserved in education. Thus, scholars from a variety of disciplines—sociology, psychology, health sciences, political science, legal studies, and social work—can assist us in reversing trends in education that continue to have devastating effects on student experiences and outcomes. What is clear from solid evidence is that these students succeed when appropriate mechanisms are in place. The Race and Education series will contribute to this tradition, centralizing those mechanisms that will help us reach our true ideal democracy. I am ready. I am hopeful that readers of the series are as well.

Welcome! #LetsDotheWork!

THE FIELD OF SCIENCE education research is often criticized by practitioners in classrooms as being disconnected from the everyday realities of working directly with young people. Practitioners consistently complain that they cannot bring the work being produced by academics into classrooms because of how it is said. For teachers, academic research seems to ignore real-life contextual factors that directly affect teaching. This circumstance, coupled with the impression that researchers seem to enjoy the esoteric nature of academic research at the expense of connecting with real people, creates a chasm between the researcher and the teacher. In general, STEM education researchers focus intently on the language of science, mathematics, and engineering in order to gain acceptance into content communities that are not invested in K–12 education. There is a misperception among academics that scientific language denotes academic rigor, and in the search to be seen as serious and rigorous they must adopt language that alienates the teacher.

Science in the City: Culturally Relevant STEM Education champions a different type of STEM education. The work challenges established ideas about what it means to engage in education research through a merging of research, personal narrative, and general observations about how the world works. In each chapter, the book's themes are anchored to the present day in a profound way. A "new era" is explored through Brown's critique of long-standing academic traditions;

how STEM education operates in the present day; and how it should work moving forward. There is a "presentness" to this work that is provocative in an era where most academic research in the field is a rehashing of what has been said or done before. Current work related to language in science discusses its variance from everyday English; however, it doesn't account for the importance of culture, creativity, or syntax in the conversation about science language. *Science in the City* probes these critical dimensions and discusses factors like *belonging* and *generational trauma* as factors to consider in STEM education. It is mind-boggling that topics so logically related to underachievement are absent in the literature, and it is powerful that they are brought to the fore and seriously considered in this book.

Brown uses accessible language to describe the problems within STEM education and shows the ways that language and context affect children who are learning science. The work offers both subtle and overt critiques of the status quo in science education, along with possible solutions. We learn about how television shows reinforce stereotypes about who can be a scientist; how different cultures define science; how science identity is shaped over time; how neutrality in science language is an impossibility; and how perceptions of "whiteness" and "blackness" play a significant role in our relationships to and perceptions of who can or cannot engage in academic science. We learn how an overarching hierarchy that exists both within and outside of STEM education equates content language to content knowledge. *Science in the City* also shows us that the language of science has been coopted by those who seek power even when they have no true command of the subject and makes the case that everyone can "do science" if there is a recognition of their entry point into the discipline.

One of the most significant offerings in the text is *disaggregate instruction* pedagogy. This is not the crux of *Science in the City*, but a powerful overture for the field offering a distinct method to good science teaching that scholars can appreciate and that teachers can follow. Brown models this powerful idea in his writing. His introduction to the concept is masterful, taking the reader through the process of understanding, self-assessing, and developing clarity; connecting to our everyday experiences; formulating it in the language of disaggregate instruction and scaffolding it to other concepts. It is through this type of work—one that models while teaching—that we transform STEM education.

When scholars and practitioners are offered details about what students need without being too prescriptive or too general, good work takes root. To make this type of substantive contribution to an area of study that hangs on tightly to its exclusionary traditions is challenging. Yet this is what this book accomplishes. *Science in the City* provides a focus on populations that have been made to feel that they do not matter by showing us why and how we STEM educators are complicit in this process. Bryan Brown convinces the field that focusing on young people feeling and sounding good—and paying attention to the details in their language and contexts—will contribute to the mastery of science content.

The new frontier in STEM education is academic work that is equally as focused on the traditional mechanisms of how the content is delivered and a concurrent consideration of the context in which it is being delivered. Brown's work spearheads this new direction through a consideration of a more robust and holistic approach to science education that retains academic rigor while holding tightly to the important humanistic element of teaching and learning. His considerations of language and content are cutting-edge and transgressive, yet in line with what many STEM educators profess to be their intention—to have all young people develop a relationship with STEM disciplines that have historically been made to be inaccessible to too many.

—CHRISTOPHER EMDIN
Associate Professor, Teachers College, Columbia University

Remembering the Power of a Story

I AM NOT A WRITER. Writing is uncomfortable for me. Despite this, I felt the need to write a book that chronicled the research I have conducted over the years. Yet I did not want use the formal style required for my research articles. I had to ask myself, "How do you want to tell the story?" That question transported me back to a story that shaped my life.

In the summer of 1994, I visited Marcus Bookstore in North Oakland, California. Behind the counter stood a young woman who I recognized from a world away. After struggling to recognize her, I realized that she had been a fellow student at Hampton University. It was disconcerting, because the two worlds of Hampton, Virginia, and Oakland, California, could not have been more different. We had a shared experience, which led to a conversation, which led to her suggesting I read Derrick Bell's book *Faces at the Bottom of The Well*. I purchased the book, but did not crack its cover until the following Thanksgiving.

I spent that Thanksgiving with my Aunt "Dimpy" King in Aliquippa, Pennsylvania. I did not go alone—I carried Bell's beautiful text with me. As I lay in my attic room, I opened what I soon discovered would be my favorite book. Bell did not simply attempt to teach his readers about race in America, he painted a story of how race mattered. He did it in an unconventional way. He simply told a story.

Bell's account of about Geneva Crenshaw's mythical travels through time and space revealed powerfully how race played a central role in the founding and sustaining of social structures in the US. But for me it did something else. His powerful and elegant portrayal of how real issues of fear and nepotism drive the racial divide in America renewed my belief in the power of a story as a way to teach. *Faces* captured my imagination, painted a picture, and pushed me to place myself in the narrative. I was no longer stuck in that attic, I was traveling through words and time to a place I had never gone before. So, as I found myself trying to write a book twenty-four years later, I felt compelled to write a story.

But the story that follows is not my story. Rather, it is the account of how I learned about the subtle, yet powerful, relationship between language, culture, and science learning. I was there, but only as a bystander. This is the story of my students, my community, and the experiences that taught me how to teach science to city kids.

This tale could not have been told without the support of the lead characters in my own narrative. Like all people, I am many things, but the roles I play most proudly are "a believer," "Cheryl's husband," "Cameron's dad," and "Simone's dad." I am forever grateful for the blessing of my Lord and savior Jesus Christ; I am truly an example of how "all things" are possible for those who believe. To be married to the most the beautiful, loving, and caring woman I have ever met continues to be a joy beyond imagination. Cheryl, your role as confidante and adviser made this text possible. Simone, I marvel at the woman you are becoming; and Cameron, the world is simply not ready for the talent you possess—it is always shark season! These emerging narratives are among the most important I have had the opportunity to witness. Their love and support are precious and extraordinary.

This research is the byproduct of generations of support that laid the foundation for me to start my own education. I have the most incredible family. John L. Brown, Barbara Brown, and Janell Brown, this book reflects years of your unwavering support. This is our story.

Finally, my desire to tell a story of science teaching is rooted in the incredible things I continue to learn from my team. Phillip Boda, Mia Hoover, Catherine Lemmi, Greses Perez, Kathryn Ribay, Matt Wilsey, and Lynne Zummo, your tireless work throughout this project made the ideas become a reality. As we explored the world of culturally relevant virtual reality, I was able to write this because of your continued commitment to excellence. For this, I am truly thankful.

In the end, the perusal of an exquisitely crafted narrative of how race shaped the realities of America laid the foundation for the experiences I recount here. It my sincere hope that as you read through these pages, you can imagine yourself in these classrooms. As you hear about how language impacts science learning, you can place yourself in the chairs of the students in the story. I hope these pages lift you to a place where all students are loved and supported because their science teachers believe that there is no barrier between their talented students' learning and the world of science. If I am lucky, working through the text in your own attic will make your desire to understand greater than your desire to be right. That is the center of *Science in the City*. It is the story of people like me, of people raised in the inner city who have a sincere desire to change the world we live in. Thank you for coming on this journey with me.

Sincerely,
Bryan A. Brown, PhD

Playing to Our Strong Suits

"When baseball is the only game in town, football
players are always playing today a weak suit.
Until eventually, they stop playing the game."

—MARY MONTEL BACON

I DRIFTED THROUGH HOURS of mundane professional development while attending my first International Baccalaureate Conference. But when I heard Dr. Mary Montel Bacon speak these words, I sat up and paid attention. I was enthralled by her energy, but confused by her message. The analogy was striking, yet so out of place. What could she mean? In the next hour, Dr. Bacon would outline a detailed, thoughtful historical narrative about why it was almost illogical to ask some children to participate in an educational system they deemed irrelevant. The point resonated deeply with me. I considered the complexity of her analogy. The point she was unpacking was that if we provide students with only one way to find success, it makes sense for them to seek success on their own terms. In the US educational system, we were selling a vision of educational success that did not make sense for many kids. Teachers were teaching science, but they forgot that we are not teaching *science*; instead, we are teaching *people*. We want the

1

people to learn science, but ultimately, we cannot act as if the people do not matter. Dr. Bacon's bold assertion suggested that if we ignore the needs of our students, they will ignore schooling as an institution.

Baseball, in Bacon's observation, represents an education that makes no accommodation for the students in the room. In a "baseball" classroom, teachers focus merely on the content. The suggestion was that it is reasonable to expect students to opt out of a system because it does not fit who they are. This system hints: "You are not valued." "What you care for is not important." "The things that motivate you have no connection to school." I was dazzled by her message—and by how it generated a shift in the crowd. What came next forever changed my vision of education.

THE GENERATIONAL EDUCATIONAL DILEMMA

What I learned that day was Mary Montel Bacon's theory of the *generational educational dilemma*; what I gained was a theoretical lens that would last a lifetime. This theory offered an enlightening lens on race and education that begged scholars to view education along a timeline. The generational educational dilemma claims that years of historical oppression have produced our current educational conditions, where inequitable education is the norm. Even after twenty-one years in education, I have yet to encounter this idea in text form. Dr. Bacon's argument is that full access to a high-quality education is something new for most African American and Latinx children—only a generation old. Take a look at the timeline in figure I.1. A college student who is prepared to graduate from college this year would be approximately twenty-two years old. That means they were likely born in 1996. But when were their parents' born? Let's assume the average person has a child by age twenty-eight. Their parents were born in 1968. That means our students' grandparents were born in 1940. And in 1940, the timeline indicates, educational opportunities for African

FIGURE I.1   Generational educational dilemma timeline

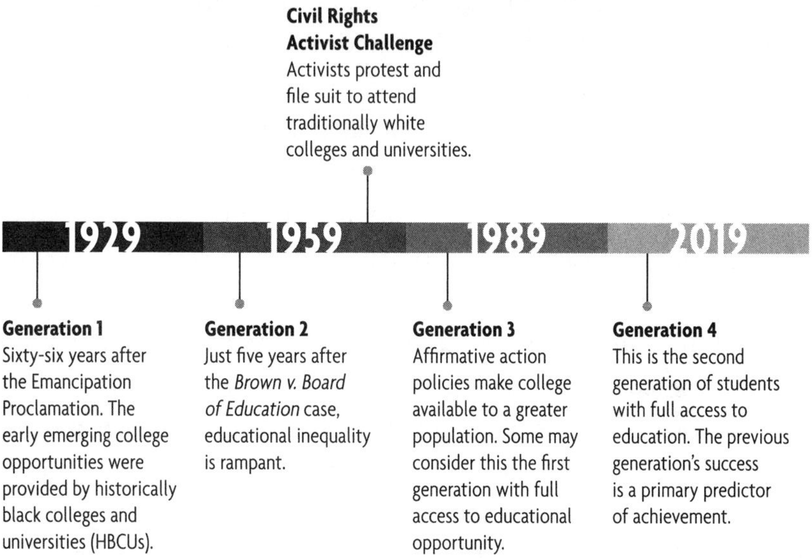

**Civil Rights
Activist Challenge**
Activists protest and
file suit to attend
traditionally white
colleges and universities.

1929   1959   1989   2019

Generation 1
Sixty-six years after
the Emancipation
Proclamation. The
early emerging college
opportunities were
provided by historically
black colleges and
universities (HBCUs).

Generation 2
Just five years after
the *Brown v. Board
of Education* case,
educational inequality
is rampant.

Generation 3
Affirmative action
policies make college
available to a greater
population. Some may
consider this the first
generation with full
access to educational
opportunity.

Generation 4
This is the second
generation of students
with full access to
education. The previous
generation's success
is a primary predictor
of achievement.

American and Latinx were little to none. African American people in the South were not allowed to go to white colleges and had limited access to high school. Aside from a small handful who attended predominately white institutions in the South, African Americans had only one option for college education, a historically black college. And pre-*Brown v. Board of Education*, such a school would likely not be able to obtain equitable physical resources and local funding.[1]

When we move to the years when our college student's parents were born, around 1966, we find the country entrenched in an epic battle for educational and civil rights. Students across the country were fighting to integrate elite educational institutions. That is, equitable educational access was clearly not yet available for African American and Latinx students.

The first assumption of the generational educational dilemma suggests that full access to a modern educational opportunity did not happen for most black and brown families until the 1970s or '80s, and that we are in the first generation of full educational rights for students of color. Now, terms like *First Gen student* are used to remind us that it is more challenging for students who do not come from affluent families with histories of college-going to make their way to a college institution. Educational structures bear the weight of their historical legacy. They reflect the privilege of some and discriminatory practices used against our forefathers, and they should never be examined in a void.

As I think about science teaching and learning in contemporary schools and communities, I think about them in this context. This book was written to help craft the narrative and paint the picture of how the psychological, sociological, and linguistic histories of oppression have made their way into contemporary science classrooms. It is intended to show the realities of years of educational disservice to communities, but it is also designed to share tried and true practices that can improve the way urban children experience science.

A CONTEMPORARY DILEMMA IN SCIENCE EDUCATION

Along with the generational educational dilemma that afflicts the US education system overall, there is a generational educational dilemma in science education as well. Unlike the dilemma framed in Bacon's analysis of the broader educational system, contemporary science education suffers from a history of stereotyping, linguistic prejudice, and cultural conflict that undermine a school's capacity to provide effective science education for all.[2] The science that is taught today reflects generations of science that was taught with a single audience in mind. This lineage now shapes the way students experience contemporary science classrooms. *Science in the City* explores the impact of this heritage.

STEREOTYPES AS DRIVING FORCES IN STEM

One of the most obvious and well-researched aspects of science's generational dilemma involves how stereotypes determine who can participate in science. Even at the time of writing, the nation's number-one comedy television program, *The Big Bang Theory*, portrays old, tired images of the science community, where the stereotype of the successful scientist is an awkward white male who lacks basic social skills.[3] The show sends a resounding message about who belongs in science.

The stereotypes about who can become a scientist do not merely exist in television, but have been reinforced for generations in the general social milieu. These stereotypes indirectly reference a perception of who should *not* be a scientist. If white, awkward men are scientists, then are cool Latinx women immediately out of the consideration? Stereotypes work this way—they frame an expectation and establish a seed of doubt for those who dare to defy them. I am not suggesting that a generationally persistent stereotype determines who can become a scientist. Instead, I am suggesting that existence of that stereotype presents invisible obstacles for those who do not fit this image. A talented African American male student who dresses like the fourth member of the hip-hop group Migos will have to question whether or not science is a real option because of this real stereotype. A young woman who lives her life as a proud feminist will have to question whether or not physics is a place for her because generations of stereotypes send her a message that she does not belong. As students of color achieve in science fields at rates we have never seen before, they are achieving under the cloud of negative stereotypes about who can become a scientist. We cannot ignore the reality of the barriers these expectations impose.

Psychologists have explored the power of these subtle interactions, which they call *social identity contingencies.*[4] Valerie Purdie-Vaughns describes this perspective by explaining how cues of social interactions produce social identity contingencies: "Certain features or cues in a setting may create the expectation that a person's treatment will be contingent on one of their social identities. Social identity contingencies are possible judgments, stereotypes, opportunities, restrictions, and treatments that are tied to one's social identity in a given setting (Steele, Spencer, & Aronson, 2002) [p. 615]."[5] A social identity contingency is the cost that people must pay for existing outside of the box.

The "judgments, stereotypes, opportunities, restrictions, and treatments" are the ways that racial stereotypes shape a students' experience in classrooms. In the case of science, our generational expectations for who can participate in STEM create an environment where students constantly have to ask the question, "Do I belong?" For example, an African American student with long dreadlocks and gold teeth in an AP chemistry class might feel the need to show people just how smart he is because he understands that the expectations of who he is do not match the model of a "good chemistry student." This is wrong, but this is a social identity contingency. The issue has additional dimensions because there are other people in the room. If the teacher and other students have never encountered a brilliant person of color who loves to wear his hair in the traditional African dreadlock, they may assume that the student is not intelligent—another stereotype. This is an additional burden the student must manage. The awkward looks or surprised faces classmates may show when they hear this young man offer a detailed and accurate answer would constitute social contingencies. And these social contingencies have a powerful impact for how people experience science classrooms.

Science in the City examines the nuances of these interactions. When students speak eloquently about scientific information in language that reflects the culture that they are from, do teachers hear their brilliance? In this text we will integrate theories of sociolinguistics, cognition, and learning to examine how generations of cultural stereotyping have allowed teachers to teach students from a position of implicit cultural bias that crosses the borders of language, culture, and cognition. We currently exist in a dynamic multicultural and multilingual society. Thus, science teachers must develop a detailed understanding of the power of culture and language in their teaching and learning interactions.

This text spends the bulk of its time examining how the language of science stands as a central gatekeeper in the interactions that produce these contingencies. As Bacon explains, we often ask students to operate in cultural environments that are simply distant from their own culture. Language often stands as this barrier. Multilingual students who flow brilliantly back and forth between Spanish, English, Khmer, and various cultural dialects are simply not afforded the ability use the intellectual resources that define their home environments.[6] This is a calamitous mistake that does two things simultaneously. First is sends a resounding message that the culture of *these* young people is not valued in science. Second, it tells the students that language and culture they are from offer no scientific value, depth, or intellectual benefit. This is simply not true and reflects our inability to understand the powerful resources of the culture that students bring with them into their science learning environments. Scholars have examined this intersection for years; however, science educators have been slow to identify how to use these linguistic and cultural resources for science teaching.[7] A vision for an empowering STEM education must recognize the value of rethinking how language, culture, and cognition shape contemporary teaching and learning. *Science in the City* explores this vital relationship.

PURPOSE AND STRUCTURE OF THIS BOOK

Science in the City was written with three primary goals in mind. First, it describes how the subtle aspects of language, race, and culture have a specific impact on students of color. It examines how the unique

nature of science teaching and learning exacerbates the conflicts experienced when race, language, and science cultures collide. Second,
it uses research to offer new evidence of the emotive and cognitive
impact of race, culture and science language. Third, this book aims to
help readers translate theory and research into meaningful pedagogical practices that are founded on research.

The book is structured in two parts. In the first part, I explore how
language and culture are vital aspects of teaching and learning from
a theoretical and pragmatic position. The second part examines how
we can use specific, well-researched teaching practices that will help
your students retain science content and see how science is a relevant
feature of their own culture.

Chapter 1 starts with story of James Meredith. It examines the
context of his integrating the University of Mississippi and examines
the notion of the *black tax*, the idea that people of color are judged
harshly and have to pay an additional "tax" to have an opportunity to
succeed. The chapter explores how language and race are intricately
connected to science learning, but how for many students of color
there is a tax to their way of community.

Chapter 2 explores how linguistic norms are established in classrooms. Although teachers and administrators arrive to classrooms
environments from diverse academic and cultural experiences, they
often fail to establish a culture where students can use their voice.
Many adopt a common linguistic norm that privilege students providing "right answers" and discourages the adoption of spaces for hybrid
language practices. The chapter explores how teachers discriminate
against students based on unstated norms about what gets said and
how language is to be used in science classrooms.

Students' science cognition and its association with the language
is the subject of chapter 3. It describes how students can offer insightful science explanations that do not rely on science language and examines the consequences when teachers fail to understand to take

into account students' cultural repertoires and ways of expressing their knowledge.

Chapter 4 is dedicated to connecting the issues of language, race, and identity to student learning. It explores theories of language and learning from both psychologists and cognitive scientists to examine how taking a cultural approach to understanding language would impact students' science learning. This chapter argues that providing students with language they can understand to begin a lesson is an essential link in their being able to successfully develop a clear conception of a phenomenon.

Chapter 5 explores a teaching approach known as *disaggregate instruction*, which focuses on addressing issues of cognition and affect in contemporary classrooms. Although it was specifically designed for teaching in science courses, disaggregate instruction concerns itself with language, first building initial cognitive understanding using students' own linguistic resources and then explicitly teaching students to use the new discourse of the lesson. When using this approach, teachers will introduce the big ideas through simple language and explicitly define the language valued in the classroom learning environment. The object is to reduce the anxiety and affective responses to complex discourse by reducing the cognitive load at the beginning.

Chapter 6 uses the story of a "hero teacher" to frame the idea of explanation as the foundation of understanding best practices for teaching and learning. It offers a number of instructional practices that help students experience the basic aspects of science ideas but focuses on developing mastery by discussing the science in culturally meaningful ways. This *generativity* approach to teaching specifically focuses on rethinking how we can use formative assessment as a tool for teaching.

In chapter 7, the story of the rise of Netflix is used to explain how excellent science teaching will require policy makers to focus on the strengths and weaknesses of contemporary STEM education.

This chapter explores how science educators must rethink our current instructional models. Unlike other disciplines, science has a dynamic set of external experts and resources. Chapter 7 explores the potential of these supplemental instructional resources. Finally, this chapter challenges educators and policy makers alike to rethink how we use technology to support science teaching. It proposes that technology can be used to enhance the cognitive and cultural experience for all students.

The simple message of *Science in the City* is that science teaching is the ultimate people business. We are not teaching a room of individuals who are the same from state to state and community to community. We have the privilege of teaching vibrant young minds who show up with a wealth of linguistic and cultural resources. To maximize their education, the next generation of STEM teachers must develop a deep understanding of how to use these resources to make science visible to these students. The point of teaching science is to provide young people with a lens that they can then use to change the world we live in. Science education is about speaking to everyone's strong suit and making sure science is among the things that feel like home.

CHAPTER 1

What Grandma and James Meredith Knew

The Black Tax

A SIMPLE IMAGE provided the inspiration for this book. One day, as I searched for a motivational photograph to serve as the desktop image for my computer, I came across an iconic image from 1962. It shows James Meredith walking into the University of Mississippi for the first time. Angry students, irate community members, and US marshals surround him.

Meredith is known as the bold and courageous integrator of Southern universities.[1] But what I saw in this image was not a reflection of a civil rights leader, but rather the picture of a young man. I tried to imagine what he was thinking during the tension-filled moments as he approached the university doors. As I considered what it must have been like to be this young man at that moment, I wondered about the type of student he had to be to endure the hostile challenge of Jim Crow America.

I imagined a young man nervous about his first day at the most elite university in his state. I imagined a young revolutionary prepared to deal with the racial slurs and hostile looks that would certainly be directed at the first African American to integrate a racially toxic environment. As I envisioned myself in his shoes, I grew increasingly amazed at the level of excellence that was inherently embedded in being James Meredith. Nervousness and doubt afflict all young students in the early days of their assimilation at high-end academic institutions, but how much greater was the challenge for a young African American man like James Meredith?

Although Meredith sat in the same classes as his colleagues and read the same books, there is no way we can consider the challenges of his colleagues in this learning environment equal to Meredith's own. Imagine reading a textbook, knowing that your classroom experience will be full of racial bias. Consider preparing for class with the full understanding that hecklers will line the hallways and streets as you make your way to lectures. Even for a military veteran like Meredith, it would be hard to bear the compounded pressure of normal academic challenges and enduring racial conflict.

How did Meredith face these dilemmas? What kinds of things did he say to prove his academic worth? How did he say them? What types of conversations did he have with the people around him? How did he negotiate the cultural norms of awkward discussions? What cues did he hear in others' voices to determine if they were friend or foe? What is incredible about James Meredith's journey is that he somehow managed these challenges, excelled, and graduated despite these additional complications of being black in a racist America. So how did a man of Meredith's background succeed despite the realities of his social quandary?

This book is not written to tell the story of James Meredith, but rather to tell the story of the price students like Meredith need to pay to earn the ears and respect of the people they come to encounter. Black people have for years described this burden as the *black tax*. The idea is simple: the success of black people has historically been accompanied by an additional price, or tax, in the form of unfair evaluations, racially biased social norms, and low expectations. The black tax was an accepted reality. Elders in the black community would often offer a gentle warning suggesting that in order for black people to succeed, they would have to be better than their white counterparts. James Anderson's seminal research on school culture described schools as places where students experienced a double taxation. He described how students of color suffered through an educational experience that was deeply unjust.[2]

The black tax is also imposed in the form of expectations about which language practices are deemed acceptable. Although this term is used widely in a colloquial sense, it is rarely applied as a theoretical lens in modern research. In reflecting on the image of James Meredith's first day of school, I am convinced that he was very aware of the challenges that lay before him. He must have been aware of how to perform academically and how to engage linguistically. He must have understood how his language was being used to measure his worth. He knew his performance would be evaluated differently. He clearly operated by the rules and principles of the black tax world he lived in. In the end, James Meredith knew what grandma knew: that being black and successful in America required additional endurance, additional patience, and a focus on clearing the additional hurdle inherent in being a member of an inequitable America.

THE BLACK TAX IN A SO-CALLED POST-RACIAL WORLD

So does the black tax apply to today's world? In a world bursting with calls for the adoption of a post-racial perspective on society, we must carefully consider how race plays a role in shaping educational opportunities for all people of color. The black tax not only tells the story of African Americans, but it also helps to frame the narrative of the challenges experienced by all non-white Americans.

However, the narrative of the black tax is dichotomous in today's society. People of color are afforded opportunities to succeed in ways never before imagined. Yet society still bears the scars of an American history of prejudice, and many continue to be exposed to poor educational environments, psychological stressors, social contingencies, and a preponderance of negative messages about who they are as American citizens. So, although opportunities for success have emerged, the poverty and inequality continue as legacies of a past where legislation created inequitable opportunities to achieve. Ultimately, as people attempt to use the current education system to obtain personal and financial freedom, they must do so despite the existing burden of unequal linguistic norms and educational environments. Collectively, these two realities are indicative of the fact that people are now able to participate in society in ways James Meredith could not have imagined. Yet, people must also recognize that access does not ultimately equate to equity.

THE MYTH OF LINGUISTIC NEUTRALITY

I start the black tax narrative by examining how language is not a neutral medium of communication and learning. When we think about schools and the way teachers and students interact, the type of language used has a profound impact on how teachers view students and how students see themselves as members of the learning community. Although the culture of US schools has changed dramatically, linguistic racism still subtly finds its way into modern classrooms, creating a double standard for students of color. This shows up in the ways cultural language practices can be viewed as deviant, deficient, and undesirable in the classroom. As a result, the cognitive potential and cultural empowerment that would be gained by allowing students to use their rich language discourses in schools is lost, and students must pay the cost of cultural assimilation, which I contend is a contemporary version of the black tax.

The language we employ is a matter of identity. Even when people speak the same language, dialect is a distinctive marker of a person's position in the world. What is intriguing about this identity game are the rules inherent in using such language. If an eighty-year-old white woman was to describe her *drip*—using a dialect common to African American teenagers—her selection of that term could be perceived in a number of ways. It could be seen as humorous if done well, but it could also be interpreted as highly offensive. I would question whether, at any point, an eighty-year-old woman could use the term and have it seen as evidence of authentic membership in the community of speakers.

In some ways, there is an economy of language use that reduces the scope of who is permitted to use a particular discourse. Catherine Prendergast makes this argument as she explores how being literate is not enough for people of color to maintain access to equitable treatment. Using a series of court cases that focus on the use of literacy tests, she makes a thoughtful thesis statement that literacy practices are white property and operate by a theory of economic availability. As more people gain access to the literacy practices, the less valuable those practices become. In other words, when black and brown people gained access to them, they lost their value in the white community. As people of color begin to earn higher scores on tests, new assessments are created. Thus, the very value of the literacy practices is deeply connected to *who* is using them.[3]

I suggest that language operates on the same grounds. If people of color have a way of communicating that is deeply rooted in their cultural history, it becomes their economic good. Linguists, in fact, argue that language practices hold value in identity maintenance and cultural pride. Joshua Fishman writes: "The joys of one's own language and ethnicity are subsequently expressed over and over again, from every corner of Europe and in every period. In modern times this feeling has been raised to a general principle, a general esthetic, a celebration of ethnic and linguistic diversity per se, as part of the very multisplendored glory of God, a value, beauty, and source of creative inspiration and inspiring creativity—indeed, as the basic human good. It is claimed that it is ethnic and linguistic diversity that makes life worth living."[4] Talking with a native Texan drawl or with a thick Boston accent can be a profound cultural experience that sustains the speaker's sense of belonging to a community.

So, what happens when cultural outsiders attempt to speak a dialect that is not their own? When a white speaker attempts to use the dialect of a Puerto Rican sub-community, two things happen. First, the hearers gain insights on who that person is as an individual. The speaker can be seen as an someone who is trying to be a member of the speech community or as someone who is disrespecting the community. Second, the language of the community becomes less pure. The very economic value of the language as a marker of identity has been cheapened because the practice has been expanded beyond the contexts of its cultural origins. I do not contend that this change is either good or bad, but it is indicative of the fact that language is not a neutral medium that can be readily selected by all who endeavor to adopt a new language or dialect. Dialect always belongs to someone, and ultimately, adopting a new dialect comes at a cultural cost.

Language philosopher Mikhail Bakhtin, in his work on the inherent nature of language, culture, and experience, highlights how language reflects deep social history: "The word in language is half someone else's. It becomes one's 'own' only when the speaker populates it with his own intentions, his own accent, when he appropriates the word, adapting it to his own semantic and expressive intention. Prior to this moment of appropriation, the word does not exist in a neutral and impersonal language . . . but rather it exists in other people's mouths, in other people's contexts, serving other people's intentions; it is from there that one must take the word, and make it one's own."[5] Considering language norms through Bakhtin's lens suggests that adopting a dialect involves drawing connections to all others who have used those words in those ways and in those contexts. This adoption of a discourse is empowering for the speaker, who can inhabit the history and culture of a word as he or she uses it. Conversely, when people use words that are not their own, they also change the inherent cultural value of those words. When race becomes the subtext, then using a word commonly used in Latinx discourse, for instance, would immediately connect the speaker to the history and culture of those words. Conversely, it could also devalue that word in the Latinx community.

So, could an eighty-year-old woman describe her style as "drippin'"? Absolutely. However, there is a price to pay. The word will never be the same, and those who held the term as property in their cultural ethos have lost a valuable tool in their linguistic repertoire. They have lost a word that was once theirs. Using a language or dialect is certainly not neutral to who the speaker is.

When we think about the culture of school and the normal discourse of science environments, we must consider how using academic language is also not culturally neutral. Using science words can serve as a mechanism for people to draw a connection to that field. Those words identify people who belong to the science community and give them value in that community. Are students who come to schools using dialects that are not valued in school assessed and evaluated with equity? Are they seen as intelligent and insightful when their explanations reflect their home culture? If we apply this lens to understanding language interactions, the linguistic norms of schools are biased. If school culture does not recognize diverse dialects as norms, then it privileges a single dialect. Therefore, students from cultures that do not use that mode of discourse must learn to adopt it—at a cost to their own comfort and culture. As a result, schools are sites of very powerful language-identity clashes. Rosina Lippi-Green explores these issues from a sociolinguistics lens, analyzing how language variation drives social identity. She documents how accents are both the source of regional and ethnic pride as well as a means of discrimination: "Much of linguistic variation is structured around social identity. Linguists know this, but non-linguists know it too, and act on it: accent becomes both manner and means for exclusion. The fact is, however, that when people reject an accent, they also reject the identity of the person speaking: his or her race, ethnic heritage, national origin, regional affiliation, or economic class. Thus, the concept of accent, so all-encompassing in the mind of the public, is a powerful one which needs to be investigated."[6] In observing how accents are not treated equally, Lippi-Green's work explodes the myth of linguistic neutrality concerning accents. As people interact in conversations, they are often unaware or unwilling to accept the implicit privileging of accents and dialects. Although people are intuitively aware of what constitutes normal discourse, we rarely challenge *whose* discourse is allowed to be the norm.

NORMING DISCOURSE

Schools are reflections of the society that designs them. As a result, they often mirror the historical and cultural norms of the societies schools are intended to prepare students to participate in. Williamson-Ige has reviewed prominent theories about the policies of black language and their association with education and concludes that the numerous lenses that frame black language practices as deviant or deficient often reflect a privileging of white norms. To support that argument, she suggests that the traditional norms of culture tend to reflect the culture of power and that language follows this same framework: "[Geneva] Smitherman (1972: 63) makes a cogent assessment of the political realities surrounding black language: 'It is axiomatic that if black people were in power in this country, Black English would be the prestige idiom.' Summing up the political ramifications a later article, Smitherman (1981: 154) continues, 'As long as we have two separate societies in contact and conflict, we're going to have two separate languages.'"[7] What is intriguing about this analysis is the idea that although language norms are generally associated with the culture of power, subcultures maintain their cultural language practices as opposed to merely adopting the norm. Said differently, people have an opportunity to sound like the mainstream, but they know that so-called mainstream language is the cultural dialect of a particular group of people. If another group of people were in power, their dialect would be the norm.

This practice of choosing whose language is considered appropriate is rooted in our understanding of the nature of stereotypes. Nailah Nasir argues that stereotypes are indexical; that is, the very nature of ascribing a stereotype is to provide an index to compare against some other group. As we use stereotypes, we by default define the norm of a group that is not mentioned.[8] For example, if the stereotype is "white men can't jump," we are subtly indexing another group without even mentioning them by name. We do not have to explain that white men can't jump but that black men can.

So what happens when one group's language practices are framed as non-academic? The obvious answer is that by contrast, we define an alternative group as having a language practice that is inherently academic. Linguists would argue that no such group exists and might note that merely writing down the discourse of white native English speakers would reveal that white discourse practices are no more academic than black ones.[9] However, if the norms of white discourse are seen as the norm of classroom conversation, we have created an indexical ranking of discourses that privileges white discourse and disenfranchises speakers of African American vernacular language, ultimately levying a tax against many minority students.

From Williamson-Ige's perspective, people can either adopt the culture of the primary power structure or reject it is as a means to sustain their cultural identity.[10] This is an age-old cultural practice that finds its roots in early America. There is a reason we do not speak with British accents today. Early Americans arrived from a diverse set of linguistic backgrounds and together developed the dialects we use today, but beyond that, sounding different from the culture of power was an empowering act that allowed early Americans to develop and sustain their own unique identity.

Just as language serves as a cue to an individual's unique identity, it also serves as the marker of ethnic identity. Although language norms are the product of privileging a particular way of communicating, people maintain the power to use their language as a symbol of group affiliation. Fishman explains how language and ethnicity are deeply connected: "[L]anguage is part of the authentic 'doing' constellation and the authentic 'knowing' constellation that are recurring assumed to be dimensions of ethnicity. Ethnic doing and knowing are more mutable and, therefore, in danger of inauthenticity. Ethnic doing is a responsibility that can be shirked. Ethnic knowing is a gift that can be withheld."[11] Fishman highlights how using language and knowing the rules of ethnicity are key components of community membership. Being a part of an ethnic group involves adopting the norms of that group as a source of pride. Language serves as a primary resource in marking ethnic group membership and as a result is a way for people to actively mark themselves as a part of a group. From a practical perspective, speaking in a dialect common to southern African Americans would be a comforting action that allows people to take pride in being a part of an ethnic group.

Where these actions become challenging is in the context of racism. When we identify types of discourse as different, we provide room for recognizing the cultural value of multiple ways of communicating. However, when we privilege a single mode of discourse as superior, we rank the relative value of ethnic dialects and commit the act of racism. Ultimately, this act prevents language from ever being a neutral medium. Some forms of discourse are seen as the property of white Americans and can only be used by non-white speakers if they are prepared to pay the cost of using that dialect.

FIRST IMPRESSIONS AND THE CONTEMPORARY BLACK TAX

As black or brown students enter modern classrooms, it is highly unlikely that they will encounter a teacher who shares their cultural or ethnic experience. This matters in ways that are often left unexplored.

In terms of linguistic neutrality and linguistic relativism, the teacher plays a central role in shaping the norms for classroom communication. This teacher is likely to arrive from an environment very different than the communities that educate the majority of African American and Latinx students. This teacher will shape what gets said, what language forms are deemed normal, and whose explanations are valued in classroom discussions. Is this teacher prepared to hear the astuteness of minority children's explanations, or will their cognitive contributions be lost in the cloud of uninformed first impressions about language? The price that many young people pay to be heard is that they must arrive in class sounding like the type of person their teacher wants them to be.

THE POWER OF FIRST IMPRESSIONS

When classroom instruction operates under the "acultural" illusion, teachers can mistakenly believe that there is a single dialect to use in classroom conversations. We operate based on our assumptions of the world, so when a cultural outsider is teaching a class full of urban students, the teacher assesses who she understands her students to be. She takes small bits of data, like the dialect students speak, and makes decisions about who these students are and what their capabilities can be.

Author Malcolm Gladwell describes how we rely on first impressions and use the information we have about people and the groups they belong to and make snap decisions about how we should characterize them. He writes about what happens when we listen to people who communicate in dialects and patterns we don't recognize:

> Chances are you'll lean forward a little less, turn away slightly from him or her, close your body a bit, be a bit less expressive, maintain less eye contact, stand a little farther way, smile a lot less hesitate and stumble over your words a bit more, laugh at jokes a bit less. Does that matter? Of course it does. Suppose the conversation is a job interview. And suppose the applicant is a black man. He's going to pick up on that uncertainty and distance, and that may well make him a little less certain of himself, a little less confident, and a little less friendly.[12]

Using the concept of "thin slicing," Gladwell demonstrates how people use tiny bits of information to make snap judgments about who people are.[13] If this lens is applied to the way language is used to interact with people, then we must consider how language serves as a primary site for snap judgments.

These judgments are not made with malicious intentions but are instead made from experience. As Gladwell notes: "Our first impressions are generated by our experiences and our environment, which means that we can change our first impressions—we can alter the way we thin slice—by changing the experiences that comprise those impressions."[14] The idea that we can change how we react to first impressions and initial assumptions about communities of people is both intriguing and problematic. When teachers arrive in urban class-rooms from different cultural backgrounds than those of their students, what types of first impressions do they have about the students' modes of communications? If these impressions are informed by their own experience, will they be equipped to hear the brilliance that is of-fered in African American vernacular discourse or from someone us-ing Spanish-accented English?

This dialect-centered dilemma is profound and indicative of the nuanced ways that race matters in contemporary classrooms. It is indeed a black tax. Although no student will ever need to be liter-ally "marshaled" into a classroom as James Meredith or Ruby Sparks were many years ago, black and brown children from urban com-munities are often faced with a contemporary black tax challenge. Schools today operate on the same dualistic principle where one type of discourse is privileged. That discourse is one deeply connected to the history and contexts of white, middle-class America. If we hope to improve students' learning and foster the development of their identities, we must equip contemporary educators with a modern understanding of the impact of linguistic norms on students' ac-cess to learning. I contend that this issue is vastly understudied and misunderstood.

Despite the years of generational progress, our incapacity as sci-ence educators to look past language produces a new version of the black tax. As our children walk into contemporary classrooms, mar-shals with angry faces are replaced by teachers who imagine children that should speak like white female college students, angry protest-ers are supplanted by curriculum materials that ignore the brilliance of black thought embedded and rich urban discourse. The tax is less obvious and soaks into students' experiences in more subtle ways, in digital media and buried as a subtext of all that happens in science classrooms. Despite its difference from past experiences, it is indeed a price to pay, and the cost is the same.

CHAPTER 2

The Cultural Cost of Organic Language Development

AS A FORMER SCIENCE TEACHER, the colloquial use of the word *organic* bothers me. Technically, everything that is carbon-based is organic. That includes all living things, anything that grows from the ground, and most genetically and chemically enhanced fruits and vegetables. However, the word has taken on a life of its own. Because words morph and their meanings change to reflect the purposes of people involved in communication, *organic* these days is often seen as synonymous with "left alone," "not manipulated," or "allowed to develop without hindrance."

It is this last meaning that gives me pause. If we allow language norms to be developed without explicit structure or design, we fall into a trap. The development of language norms is many things, but "organic" in this sense is certainly not one of them. Ultimately, all language exchanges are informed by histories and contexts that explicitly define them.

Although some would consider the US a nation where language practices have changed dramatically in the last century, there are aspects of our current interactions that have not varied much. Close your eyes and think for a moment about what a "smart" person sounds like. Hear that person saying something profound and interesting. I would assume that this speaker would be doing two things. First, he or she would be saying something additive or generative. Our general conceptions of what counts as an intelligent statement tend to be the expression of a new ideas or one that deviates from the accepted norm. It is the novelty of the idea that grabs our attention. Second, what is said must be couched in the dialect that we are expecting. Pattern, pace, and tone matter in our imagined construct of what counts as intelligent. So, in your imagination, did this intelligent statement include a lisp, a stutter, or a thick Southern accent? The choice is completely yours. However, our conceptions of what intelligence sounds like are deeply cultural and profoundly ethnic. The irony is that although the US is alive with cultural and intellectual change, the way many of us conceive of intelligence is informed by persistent stereotypes about what intelligent identities sound like.

The question that is central to this chapter is, *Who establishes those norms and how do they impact what happens in the classroom?* To answer this question, Dell Hymes offers us the notion of *communicative competence*. The idea is that learning a language does not equate to being competent in the language. Words are contextual and find their meaning when and how they are used. Thus, becoming competent in a language form occurs when individuals not only master the words but also become rooted in the cultural significance of what it means to use those words in context.[1]

We intuitively learn these rules and use them to guide our conception of what discourse seems normal. So, to return to the example of sounding smart, we must recognize that over time people learned who counted as smart, and made the discourse of this imagined "smart" person the normative discourse of intelligence. Unfortunately, it is the culture of power and the customs associated with that culture that determine the linguistic norms that signal intelligence. This norm presents a challenge in classrooms where the intelligent are often un-heard because their thoughtful discourse that is not recognized as in-telligent by teachers who communicate in jargon-filled lectures that reflect their own vision of intelligent discussion. In either case, a lot is lost in translation because the norms of how we speak are unspoken, nonintentional, and culturally biased.

A case in point comes from a non-academic discourse exchange. Just moments after Florida State University won the incredibly close 2014 NCAA national championship football game versus Auburn University, FSU's star quarterback, twenty-year-old Jameis Winston, was interviewed by a reporter. The dialogue went like this:

> REPORTER: You've got 1:15 to go in the game, final drive, what did you tell your teammates around you?
>
> JAMEIS WINSTON: I said, "Guys, we did not come here for no reason." I said, "Guys, this is ours, man." All the adversity we went through the first few quarters, it was ours to take. And like . . . I been saying, "We control our own destiny." And those men looked me in my eyes and they said, "We got this, Jameis." . . . I said "Are you strong?" They said, "I'm strong, if you are strong." "So," I said, "We strong then."
>
> REPORTER: After struggling through the first half, what was the biggest adjustment you made at halftime?

This account of how Winston's team managed to score in the final moments of an extraordinary football game is rich in its narrative prose and expressions of leadership. Although a mere red-shirt freshman, Winston was known as an incredible team leader. He had a custom of sprinting to the entrance of the field before and after each game so he can shake the hand of every teammate. Telling his teammates "We control our own destiny" or sharing how he expressed to

his teammates that they could be strong because he was strong reflects the leadership narrative of this young man.

What emerged as interesting was public reaction to this interview.
Many deemed Winston's account to be unintelligent and not befitting
a college quarterback. Figure 2.1 shows a tweet from the mother of
the University of Alabama's quarterback, AJ McCarron. In response
to Winston's post-game interview, Dee Dee McCarron commented:
"Am I listening to English?"

This question launched an avalanche of similar negative commen-
tary about Winston's intelligence and "incorrect" use of English in
the post-game interview. After receiving a barrage of criticism, Dee
Dee McCarron quickly deleted the initial tweet and apologized (see
figure 2.2).

The viral response agreeing with McCarron's initial tweet was
countered with a flood of tweets praising Winston's interview, including tweets by prominent athletes Reggie Bush and LeBron James
(figure 2.3).

FIGURE 2.1   Public tweet regarding post-game interview

Dee Dee McCarron @DeeDeeBonner

Am I listening to English?

1/7/14, 12:09 AM

FIGURE 2.2   McCarron's apologetic tweet

Dee Dee McCarron @DeeDeeBonner

Any1 that knows our family knows we r far from racist. My tweet was
not in anyway meant that way. I sincerely apologize if it offended any1

1/7/14, 1:39 AM

FIGURE 2.3   LeBron James and Reggie Bush's tweets

LeBron James @KingJames

UN-Freaking-believeable interview by Jameis!! Just shows part of the reason why he's SPECIAL!

1/7/14, 12:11 AM

Reggie Bush @ReggieBush

Love listening to this dude Jameis Winston talk after games! Walks and talks like a true champion! A great role model for kids to look up to

1/7/14, 12:10 AM

The storm surrounding this interview revealed a fascinating discourse about the rules for public conversation. The question that grabbed my attention was, How could some be so inspired and others be so disparaging of the same words? For me, the interview suffered from the weight of differing, unstated expectations of "organic" language. What should a hero sound like? What discursive style should an obviously intelligent and thoughtful young man use minutes after winning the most important game of his life? Tired, out of breath, and overflowing with excitement, Jameis Winston was asked a question. He answered it thoroughly, thoughtfully, and with great zeal. So how could someone hear it and ask, "Am I listening to English"?

What if Winston spoke with a thick "good-ole-boy" Southern accent? Would the grammatical correctness of his answers be questioned? Would his use of nonstandard linguistic structures be seen as down-home, authentic, refreshing? The challenge of the immediate critical reaction to his discourse is that there is a direct link between his speech patterns and the racial identity associated with using that dialect. The way he spoke in that interview was immersed in the cultural history of where he came from and the groups he belonged to—and entirely fitting.

This is a matter of imagination and unstated "organic" norms. Those who criticized Winston seemed to expect him to sound like a news broadcaster. Perhaps the expectation was that he should speak in a five-sentence-paragraph style, complete with topic sentence, supporting details, and succinct summary. Some went so far as to suggest that most large institutions hire media directors to teach their athletes how to speak to the media. Were his critics justified in feeling that their expectations had been violated? For me, the answer is a resounding *no*. In that moment, he sounded like an excited twenty-year-old African American man from Alabama. He broke the linguistic norms that he used when he was interviewed in other contexts. He broke the linguistic norms that allowed him to earn his high school degree and write in the mythical standard of "academic English." What he did was speak in a way that would surely motivate and connect with a team of eighteen- to twenty-three-year-old Southern football players. The problem is neither how he spoke nor his capability to speak. The problem was his critics placing unstated expectations on him. He was being evaluated based on a norm that was never clearly stated and simply does not exist. There is no established norm for how he was supposed to speak in that moment, but he was certainly being evaluated based on what people expected to hear.

Why talk about football interviews in a book about classroom learning? Because we do the same thing in our classrooms. When we listen to students, we listen to them with the expectation of a linguistic norm that is often inauthentic, decontextualized, and based on fictitious models of normality. When you ask a child from inner-city Boston to answer a question about her knowledge of a plant's energy needs, I would not expect her to speak with the clarity and vocabulary of Bob Costas, Barbara Walters, or Tom Brokaw. Rather, I would expect that child to use examples, narratives, and words that reflect the voice of the community in which she built her knowledge. More specifically, the student's tone, pacing, and grammatical norms are more likely to reflect her neighborhood background than the so-called academic norm.

Imagine an urban classroom in any major metropolitan city in the United States of America. I would expect the classroom to be full of African American and Latinx American students who engage in hybrid discourse practices that integrate African American Vernacular discourse and Spanglish in a diversity of ways. I would also expect that this same classroom would be taught by a white female who is not from that community and uses a dialect of English that is different than that used by her students. For her, who sounds intelligent? When her children speak, do they use the language of their neighborhood or adopt a more school-specific alternative? Either way, a severe language-identity problem emerges. Just as in the case of Jameis Winston, no one explicitly establishes a norm for the way people are supposed to speak. We tend to leave the expectation of how we are supposed to speak and what dialects are valuable as a hidden sub-curriculum. This inability to establish an explicit norm means that everyone enters the classroom with his or her own sense of what counts as normal. The result of this vague "organic" norming is that it produces many instances where students are misunderstood and teachers speak to students in ways that the students have difficulty making sense of. Together, this failure to explicitly articulate what dialect we should use on our way to learning produces a classroom crippled by clashing cultures. Therefore, allowing language to "organically" develop ultimately privileges few and creates cultural barriers for many others.

A FAILURE TO UNDERSTAND, A FAILURE TO BE UNDERSTOOD

When teachers arrive in classrooms, they have a great deal of power in determining the norms of classroom discourse. Some encourage loud classrooms where students debate ideas and explore topics in rich, detailed discourse. Others focus on classroom management; that is, keeping all of the students quiet so the teacher can do their best job of telling them what they need to know. This type of classroom becomes a game show of sorts, where students play what my dear colleague Jean Lythcott calls "Guess What's in My Head?" The goal is to say the correct answer when the teacher asks a question.

Unfortunately, this type of talk is antithetical to students learning, as content is filtered through the teacher alone. Ironically, since students are supposed to arrive in classrooms not knowing the topic being taught, asking students for answers in the "Guess What's in My Head?" game goes directly against fostering a productive learning environment. In fact, this type of discourse practice guarantees that only two types of people get an opportunity to speak: teachers themselves and the students who know the answers. This fundamentally ensures that those who need to discuss an idea in order to gain clarity never get an opportunity to express their understanding.

Teachers operate classroom discourse this way because it is the way they themselves experienced classroom language norms. It is a relic of centuries of education and is how many university classrooms have operated since the 1800s. In teachers' minds, the pedagogy reflects education at its highest level, and it replicates the culture they are familiar with.

For years, scholars have explored and critiqued this type of discourse, described as either initiation-response-evaluation (IRE) or initiation-response-feedback (IRF) modes of talk.[2] In the IRE approach, the teacher tightly controls who speaks and evaluates students' contributions to the discussion as either right or wrong.[3] This mode of classroom talk, where teachers offer students opportunities to share the right answers, effectively establishes a detail-oriented system of behavior where teachers seek those contributors who have exactly what they are looking for: a correct answer spoken in a language that the teacher wants to hear.

In the late 1970s and early 1980s, scholars offered comprehensive analyses of how this mode of discourse shaped classroom learning opportunities. In reviewing this early literature, Waring describes the IRE approach to classroom discourse by detailing just how systematic and nuanced this mode of classroom discourse can be:

> A central structure in classroom discourse is the IRF sequence (teacher initiation–student response–teacher feedback; (Sinclair & Coulthard, 1975) or IRE, where E stands for Evaluation (Mehan, 1979). According to Wells (1993), "if there is one finding on which learners of classroom discourse agreed, it must be the ubiquity of the three-part exchange structure (p. 1)." Varying views have been put forward regarding the value of IRF for learning (e.g., Hall, 1998; Nystrand, 1997; Seedhouse, 1996; van Lier, 2000; Wells, 1993). The current project joins this conversation by offering a detailed look into the role of a particular type of IRF in a homework review activity and by showing how this machinery of IRF may become relaxed or suspended.[4]

The IRF discourse mechanism in classrooms is deeply rooted in the cultural ethos of the United States, as it resonates with many of us as a common educational experience. The 1986 film *Ferris Bueller's Day Off* provides a vivid example. In a scene parodying a typical high school classroom, an economics teacher attempts to engage in IRF discourse about the concept of voodoo economics but gets little support from his students:

TEACHER: In the House of Representatives, in an effort to alleviate the effects of . . . Anyone?

TEACHER: The Great Depression passed the . . . Anyone?

TEACHER: The Hawley-Smoot Tariff Act . . . which raised or lowered . . . ?

TEACHER: Raised tariffs in an effort to collect more government
 revenue. Did it work?

TEACHER: Anyone know the effects?

TEACHER: It did not work, and the United States sank deeper
 into the Depression. Today, we have a similar debate over
 this . . . Anyone know what this is?

TEACHER: Anyone seen this before?

TEACHER: The Laffer curve. Anyone know what this says?

TEACHER: It says that at this point . . . on the revenue curve,
 you will get exactly the same amount of revenue as at this
 point. Does anyone know what Bush called this . . . ?

TEACHER: Anyone? Something-*doo* economics?

TEACHER: Voodoo economics.[5]

In this exchange, the teacher offers eleven questions and answers
all of them himself. This iconic exchange resonates powerfully with
many of us because of its close resemblance to our own experience.
We have sat in classes and listened to a teacher have a conversation
with himself under the pretense of teaching something of interest.
We have sat dazed and confused like the kids in the film's classroom.
It's no wonder that Ferris Bueller needed a day off from the grinding
monologue of IRE classroom discourse.

So how does the "Guess What's in My Head?" game of IRE shape
opportunities to learn in contemporary classrooms? Although the
example is extreme, the excerpt from *Ferris Bueller* highlights how
taking an organic approach to language learning where the norms
of academic language acquisition are not explicitly defined creates
a scenario where learning is inhibited by the dual failures of IRE instruction and the impact of race, culture, and language. In one way,
adopting the IRE approach to classroom talk prohibits the teacher
from providing students an opportunity to understand the primary

idea being expressed. Together, a failure to critically restructure academic talk limits the true power of talking to learn.

FAILURE TO UNDERSTAND

One of the biggest challenges of these organic, undefined environments of academic talk is that students are moving from classroom to classroom and enduring hour-long sessions of IRE talk. They perceive this type of academic discourse to be normal, but is it effective? I would argue that one of its primary limitations is that it produces classroom conversations where students are met with a barrage of complex ideas and terminology in ways that fundamentally inhibit their ability to understand the concepts being taught. This is particularly challenging in science classrooms, where students are being introduced to new science ideas that are explained in dense academic jargon.

When language norms are left unexplored, the classroom discussions that should be used to introduce new ideas to students become overly complex exchanges of academic terms. The default mode of communication is the classroom lecture, where new concepts and the terms used to define them are hurled at the students at great speed. If the students have an initial understanding of the concept, they may have a chance to understand and apply the new terms. But those who are unfamiliar with the subject may be left confused by the terminology.

Jay Lemke examines how this construct explicitly affects science educators. He suggests that the problem is not merely a problem of teacher talk, but also a problem associated with the complex nature of science language: "The meanings of sentences are not made up out of the meanings of words. We must arrive at both simultaneously by fitting words and their semantic relations within the sentence to some thematic pattern and the relations among its thematic items. And where do we find thematic patterns? They are part of the common ways of speaking about a subject that we have heard, read, and used countless times in speech and in writing. It is only when we meet and unfamiliar pattern that we have trouble making sense of sentences."[6]

Lemke's assertion that language is not simply an issue of knowing words but rather understanding how those words represent concepts that are inherently connected to each other is a powerful one. These connections, or thematic patterns, are learned through a person's lived experience, so when we play the "Guess What's in My Head?" game and ask students to share their knowledge while we bombard them with "correct" answers, we are obviously not putting students in the best situation to learn.

When we teach this way, we place students at a severe disadvantage. We speak to them in a language that is nearly foreign to them and expect them to understand it. We place them in jeopardy if we naively validate the accurate science responses of the few and interpret the silence of the many as ignorance. This failure to recognize the audience and their linguistic and cultural resources is a direct result of allowing the language norms of the classroom to remain organically undefined.

Imagine two people interacting for the first time in a multilingual city like Montreal. If the speaker is a bilingual French-Canadian who switches readily from French to English based on the audience and circumstance and the listener is a monolingual US native, what would we expect the speaker to do when asked for directions? I would certainly expect the speaker to answer in English and assess the questioner's familiarity with the area to find an appropriate level of explanation to best insure he arrives at his destination. Unfortunately, contemporary classrooms are largely led by teachers who make no such affordance. They merely speak science without considering how to ensure that their students understand the concept being taught.

This analogy highlights how the nuanced nature of learning the language of science deserves serious treatment by both teachers and science education researchers. Although students in science classrooms need to learn and understand academic language, few teachers understand the complexity of imparting that knowledge. Jerry Wellington and Jonathan Osborne explore the relationship between science learning and science literacy practices and offer an astute analysis of the relationship between words in colloquial and canonical form:

> As Jay Lemke (1990) argues, the language of science adopts a range of features which children will find peculiar. It avoids colloquial forms; it uses unfamiliar technical terms such as "mitosis" and "meiosis" and familiar words such as "energy," "force" and "power" in unfamiliar contexts. It avoids personification and the use of metaphoric and figurative language. In doing so, it attempts to be serious and dignified and much of it is devoted to answering questions such as "what kinds of things exist?," how do we know?," and "how does it happen?"[7]

Wellington and Osborne's description of science language as "technical," "peculiar," "serious," and "dignified" offers a vision of the language that is impersonal and specific. The lack of colloquial forms, personification, and metaphor create a type of linguistic exchange wherein teachers are not adjusting the language to meet the needs of the students. The primary responsibility of adjusting to the mode of language being used is left solely to the student. The result is that students are placed in a situation where developing a detailed understanding of concepts is extraordinarily challenging. This dilemma is the byproduct of allowing the language-learning strategy of the classroom to emerge "organically" as opposed to teaching science language as if it were a foreign language to be learned, applied, and used regularly.

A FAILURE TO BE UNDERSTOOD

Another issue with leaving language norms unaddressed is that it limits the teacher's ability to understand student cognition. As people move through the world, they gain insight and knowledge about the world through a variety of contexts, largely grounded in the culture in which they learned the information. One could reasonably expect that the language that serves to frame their knowledge is the same language that serves to shape the culture and identity for the same group of people. Therefore, one could expect that the knowledge students develop outside of the classroom environment, is explicitly rooted in their culture. Undefined language norms create problems in the classroom not only by inhibiting students' ability to understand what is being taught, but by creating an environment that inhibits teachers from recognizing students' knowledge—because it is not expressed in the language teachers expect. So, ironically, by not adjusting the language to meet students' needs, teachers are not meeting *their own* needs—to be understood so as to successfully teach science.

This failure of teachers to understand the students is not merely a matter of seeing the world in binary "rights" and "wrongs." Rather, it is rooted in teachers' inability to see the knowledge the students have merely because they are looking for the "right" answer communicated in the "right" language. The question then becomes: *What is a right and a wrong answer?*

For example, a student describing photosynthesis may give a detailed explanation of how the air enters and leaves through tiny holes in the leaf or how the sunlight travels to the plant's leaves. But the student may never mention the inverse relationship between photosynthesis and respiration. He may never mention how photons are eventually used to convert carbon dioxide into glucose. He may never mention how oxygen is released into the atmosphere. Yet the description is essentially comprehensive and correct.

We must engage in a critical examination of how knowledge is represented. In my own work, I found that concepts could be eloquently explained when students described scientific phenomena without attempting to incorporate complex science discourse. To return to the photosynthesis example, students have described how air enters into the small pockets on the bottom of the leaf while never using the word *stomata*. The challenge is whether or not these students' true understanding of the process of photosynthesis can be made visible to a teacher who does not learn how to disaggregate language and concept.

If we fail to recognize the diverse nature of language and cognition, students who bring a wealth of knowledge but communicate it in vernacular language will never be heard because the nature of classroom conversations privileges only one type of communication. We will never hear the informed insights many students have to offer because we are looking for "scientific" answers communicated in "scientific" discourse.

To add complexity to this challenge, we must consider how the use of complex language is also associated with cultural intimidation. As I have noted, language is not neutral to race, gender, and culture. Our identities are shaped through our language. Lippi-Green, in her examination of language, culture, and identity, offers a vision of how language and identity are deeply connected: "Language, a possession all human collectives have in common, is more than a tool for communication of facts between two or more persons. It is the most salient way we have of establishing and advertising our social identities."[8] The idea that people "advertise" and "establish" their identity through language is pertinent to classroom learning in powerful ways. If students are left to negotiate the complexity of learning concepts while simultaneously learning the complex language of science, their identities are also in jeopardy.

If we imagine urban students who use language to mark themselves as members of their communities, this dilemma becomes clear. For example, students raised in Los Angeles's gang neighborhoods who greet each other as "Cuz" or "Blood" exemplify Lippi-Green's idea about how language advertises who we are. If we consider how these students use slang and Los Angeles–specific terms to act out their communities' racial and cultural norms, should we be surprised when they express discomfort with using the language of science? Too often, educators assume that they can quickly assimilate to the adoption of terms like *mitosis, chromatid, centrioles,* and *chromosome* with no cultural cost. Viewing the situation through Lippi-Green's lens, however, would suggest that students would be advertising and establishing an alternative identity by using these science terms.

Ultimately, I would fully expect that, unless cued to do otherwise, students would communicate their knowledge in a discourse that reflects their cultural and ethnic identities. If teachers do not explicitly create an alternative discourse community, these demonstrations of knowledge may be fundamentally invisible to teachers who have never considered how to view students' cognition beyond the application of scientific jargon.

This point of this chapter is not to criticize or discourage the use of science dialect but rather to highlight how a culture-free, or "organic," approach to understanding language puts students in jeopardy. We cannot allow science language to be seen as "organic." It allows culture and identity to move to the foreground and fundamentally limits learning. Allowing language to organically develop generates a dichotomous dilemma. In one way, not developing a language-learning approach prevents teachers from being understood. In another way, it limits a teacher's ability to understand the knowledge the students bring with them to the learning environment.

CHAPTER 3

Linguistic Relativity and Intelligent Misunderstandings

WHEN I WAS A TEENAGER, people would often pay me compliments that insulted me at the same time. I later borrowed a term I heard from a comedian to explain this experience—*complidiss*, a hybrid of *compliment* and *diss*. The idea is simple: there are times when people compliment you, but the subtext of that compliment is a comparison to a very poor expectation. To complidiss someone is to offer them shallow praise, whether the message is intentional or not.

People experience a variety of complidisses in their everyday interactions. For example, someone can praise your fashion choice by saying "Your clothes look nice today." They may compliment your correspondence skills by writing "I really appreciate your choice of words on your e-mail this time. Great job." In both of these examples, the contingent phrases *today* and *this time* imply the comparison on which the remark is based. The compliment is that you selected an appropriate choice of clothes and words. The diss is that those selections are only good compared with your usual appearance or performance.

This passive-aggressive way to communicate also finds its way into educational environments. As a teenager, I experienced complidisses regularly as teachers, parents, and administrators evaluated my academic identity. As early as middle school, teachers would express how impressed they were that I was performing so well in the advanced academic courses while still appearing to be a "regular" African American boy. In other words, I was upsetting their expectations that African American boys should not earn As in advanced mathematics and writing courses. At the same time, I was upsetting another expectation that, if I did earns As, I should not also engage in the activities that were deemed normal for African American boys—playing basketball, freestyle rhyming, and hanging out with all–African American social groups during lunch hours. I somehow stood as a contradiction to the expectation and was rewarded with a complidiss.

In terms of language, learning, and science education, I contend that there is synergy between the fundamental assumptions behind a complidiss and the notion of linguistic relativity in science learning. In the same way that my teachers' expectations led them to be surprised by my academic performance, our expectations about students' knowledge and the language that represents that knowledge are based on similarly faulty assumptions. If we fail to consider how multiple language types can represent science knowledge, we will profoundly underestimate what students actually know.

Unrealistic expectations about language challenge students even before teaching begins. As students enter science classrooms, they are not expected to know the content being taught, so teachers often use pre-assessments and ask formative assessment questions to gain a sense of what they do know. And they tend to expect students to express their understanding of science concepts using science discourse and terminology.

There are two problems with this. First, there is no reason students should know these terms—the language is part of the content that will eventually be taught to them. Second, if students have learned about the content in another social context, it is likely that they learned it in words that are not the science terms used in the classroom. For example, in a science lesson about chemical bonding, a teacher may ask students about the differences between polar and non-polar bonding. If students' knowledge about polarity came from their experience with batteries, to them *polar* may simply mean "opposite sides." If students respond by using a battery as an example, but fail to explicitly discuss the nature of the shared electrons, is their answer right or wrong? Having a binary vision of right and wrong answers does not take into account the idea that students may hold rich science understanding in everyday language, creating an environment of low expectations.

The unrealistic expectation that students should know science ideas and express them in science language could be corrected if examined through the lens of *linguistic relativity*. All students know things. However, they may not express their knowledge in academic language. If we accept that science ideas may be represented in both science language and everyday language, a different vision of our students may emerge. Instead of being surprised by a student who phenotypically is associated with low expectations but demonstrates sophisticated science knowledge, we would begin to see the types of knowledge that all students have. If we change our vision of knowledge from the simple, binary "right" and "wrong" and the "science language only" frameworks that pervade the classroom, a different vision of our students may emerge where complidisses may become a thing of the past. The remainder of this chapter explores the concept of linguistic relativity and students' intelligent misunderstanding through an exploration of a few unique cases.

STUDENTS' KNOWLEDGE IS NOT CONFINED TO SCIENCE LANGUAGE

If teachers are going to develop students' science knowledge with depth, it will require a recalibration of their knowledge of pedagogical content. Most conceptions of pedagogical content knowledge are concerned with what teachers know about science concepts—developing analogies about the concepts, understanding appropriate examples of concepts, knowing which labs and activities best illustrate concepts, understanding which technologies are best suited for teaching, and understanding students' preconceptions of the phenomena explored. However, scholars need to add issues of linguistic relativity to our conversations about pedagogical content knowledge.

The concept of linguistic relativity is borrowed from sociolinguistic research on culture and discursive power.[1] The essential premise is that the language individuals use frames their cognitive capacity. The idea was hotly debated for years. Eve Clark credits the origins of the discussion of relativity and cognition to the now largely debunked Sapir Whorf hypothesis, which "states that (1) languages vary in their semantic partitioning of the world; (2) the structure of one's language influences the manner in which on perceives and understands the world; (3) therefore, speakers of different languages will perceive the world differently."[2] This premise changed the field's fundamental assumptions about how language and thought mattered. As people attempted to apply this framework, there were unfortunate applications of the theory that deemed minority students deficient in their cognitive potential. Over the years, the notion of linguistic relativism and its synonym *linguistic determinism* were seen as lacking conceptual depth and accuracy. The argument is that our understanding of language and thought in science teaching is oversimplified and does not represent the true relationship of language and cognition. Lera Boroditsky offers an explanation of how the early versions of the Whorfian view of language defined the relationship between language and thought:

> The doctrine of Linguistic Determinism—the idea that thought is
> determined by language—is most commonly associated with the

writings of Benjamin Lee Whorf. Whorf, impressed by linguistic diversity, proposed that the categories and distinctions of each language enshrine a way of perceiving, analyzing, and acting in the world. Insofar as languages differ, their speakers too should differ in how they perceive and act in objectively similar situations (Whorf, 1956). This strong Whorfian view—that thought and action are entirely determined by language—has long been abandoned in the field.[3]

As Boroditsky notes, the narrow view that language and thought predict each other no longer has much currency. Instead, it has been replaced by perspectives that take a more expansive approach. Today, linguistic relativity refers to conceptualization of language as a platform through which ideas are represented by words. However, these words can come from a diversity of dialects, languages, and cultures. Additionally, their meanings are non-static, synonymous, and constantly changing as people alter them meet their intellectual needs.

In this way, words are metaphors for ideas. They label, compare, and contrast ideas by connecting ideas to their origins. Words are extremely malleable and fundamentally find their value in the agreed-upon mutual meaning between speakers. When the words available to speakers are not adequate, speakers create new words or alter the existing words so that they can expand and do more. As a construct, linguistic relativity allows us to examine how ideas can have multiple representations that may be culturally different but conceptually similar. More importantly, training a linguistic relativity lens on students' knowledge would allow us to see the depths of what students truly understand.

So how does linguistic relativity help inform our work on the teaching and learning of science? If we look at what people know in their community context, we must assess the relationship between their language and the concepts they are describing. We should expect that students' knowledge might not be framed in science language. Said differently, we should expect students to know some things, and when they share their knowledge, we should expect to hear that knowledge communicated in culturally specific language as well as science terminology. Knowledge is not reduced to a single set of simple words but can exist beyond this simplistic conception of language. As a result, a true conception of pedagogical content knowledge is one that is rooted in an understanding of how language and cognition are intricately connected.

BIG D'ANDRE AND METABOLISM

To move this discussion from an abstract to a more pragmatic context, I would like to recount the story of Big D'Andre.[4]

D'Andre Hampton was a junior in an urban high school in Oakland, California. At 6'1" and 305 pounds, he was a dominant force on the football field and looking forward to a college football career. (He was eventually named an All-American and went on to play Division 1 football at the local university.)

I have a tradition of teaching in the schools where I am working on professional development projects. Demonstrating the practices I will eventually use for training helps to build rapport with teachers I am working with. In this instance, I was illustrating how to use a particular type of lesson planning by teaching a lesson on metabolism. To provide a context to think about catabolic and anabolic metabolism, I decided to discuss body size and marathon runners.

To start the discussion, I asked, "Has anyone here ever seen a marathon runner on TV? Has anyone ever seen a fat marathon runner?" Hoping to spark a discussion about physical activity and metabolic activity, I invited students to offer a number of explanations. Some offered descriptions rooted in understanding the role of sweat. D'Andre, however, offered a unique explanation of metabolism by saying

> Naw! It's like this. It's like if you set a block of ice out. Out on the curb. The ice don't just melt. First, it just turns into water. Then, the water it disappears into steam. It's like that. It don't be no fat marathon runners because when they run, they melt the fat and they body use the fat and it burns off.

D'Andre's account is an example of how linguistic relativity can inform teaching and learning in science. A simple binary analysis of whether he is right or wrong would make his knowledge invisible. Technically, he was wrong, but looking beyond mere words reveals a beautiful and deeply accurate narrative about metabolism. To assess what he really knows, we must make careful decisions about which types of discourse reflect accurate cognitive understanding.

Although his explanation does not include critical metabolic scientific terms like *catabolism, anabolism, glucose,* and *calorie,* he does create a vibrant picture that is rooted in vernacular discourse to represent the basic physical stage changes in catabolic metabolism. Is his answer correct? The lens we use to make sense of his knowledge determines how we answer this question.

If we operate on a dichotomous scale of answers being either inherently correct or incorrect, then D'Andre's answer is incorrect. However, when we switch our lens to one of linguistic relativity, we can recognize how valuable D'Andre's use of melting ice as an analogy can become. He describes how ice experiences a phase change that is similar to the physical and chemical change that fat undergoes. Although not perfect, his description of ice melting into water and ultimately evaporating into gas does relate to body fat being catabo-lized into triglycerides, then to glucose, which is used for energy. He does not draw the parallels between his explanation and the scientific alternative, but he does offer his classmates a powerful cognitive re-source—a vivid way of thinking of a component of the metabolic pro-cess. If his teacher operates from a lens that values linguistic relativity, she would be able to draw the parallels between his contribution and the goal of understanding how metabolism operates.

There are a number of ways to interpret the meaning of D'Andre's statement, "It don't be no fat marathon runners because when they run, they melt the fat and they body use the fat and it burns off," and when he says "They melt the fat," he could be suggesting that fat is lit-erally melted away through intense exercise. An alternative interpre-tation would be that he does understand the metabolic use of fat for energy purposes and its relative association to the intake of calories. Either way, it is clear that he understands that there is a connection between physical activity and the use of fat for energy. So again I ask, is he right or is he wrong?

A better question to consider is what is gained by using a linguis-tic relativity lens and what is lost by not doing so. When considering what is to be gained from this approach, the teacher may be able to affirm the merit of D'Andre's answer by highlighting the *components* of the answer that are accurate and the useful nature of his analogies. Imagine the difference it would make in students' lives if the teacher can validate what they know as opposed to telling them they are sim-ply right or wrong, or concentrating on what they *don't* know. We can also recognize how analogies are selected based on their accessibility. In this case, D'Andre used an analogy that he knew would resonate with his fellow students. If the teacher recognizes and uses the anal-ogy, there is an opportunity to begin instruction using an accessi-ble image that is based on students' own cultural experiences. So, in many ways, using a linguistic relativity lens allows the teacher to use the culturally relevant knowledge that students bring to classroom in meaningful ways.

On the other hand, his answer is not scientifically accurate. Nevertheless, it can be used as a pathway toward helping students truly understand the concept. The ultimate goal of science learning is to understand the concepts and to learn the science discourse associated with them. In this excerpt, the language of the discussion is purely vernacular and does not apply the language of science. Would it be reasonable to expect a seventeen-year-old African American from a crime-ridden neighborhood to inject science discourse into his explanation without being prompted to do so? If he did this, what cultural consequences would ensue? His selection of discourse may have offered the students listening a great resource because they are developing an initial cognitive understanding of catabolic metabolism in a discursive style that they are familiar with. If D'Andre were to offer an explanation that was rich with terms like *catabolic metabolism*, *glucose*, *triglycerides*, and *phase change*, they may have lost the initial meaning. In doing this, he may have also lost part of his cultural identity. This example conveys that taking a binary approach to science knowledge makes students' existing cultural knowledge fundamentally invisible (see table 3.1).

What can we learn from D'Andre's story? For me, his is a story of expectations. If the teacher expects to hear scientific knowledge expressed in science language, she may be deeply disappointed. If, however, she approaches, something like D'Andre's answer through a linguistic relativity lens, then the richness of students' knowledge can now become a resource for teaching and learning. Unfortunately, this is difficult and will require teachers to rethink how science is associated with vernacular and canonical language. This alteration in scientific knowledge is both complex and necessary.

TABLE 3.1   D'Andre Hampton discussing metabolism

Context	Speaker	Quote	Analysis
Teacher introduces the context	Teacher	So here's the deal. By the end of the day we will be able to provide a clear explanation of this problem. Here's the problem. Has anyone here ever seen a marathon runner on TV (hands raise). Has anyone ever seen a fat marathon runner?	• Teacher uses colloquial question to ask students to consider how exercise burns fat.
Teacher fielding potential answers	Ryland	Yeah. Oprah!	• A student attempts to make a joke.
		She's not fat. And I am talking about people who race in marathon's all the time. Has anyone ever seen a fat marathon runner? (*no response*) So here's the question: Why is it that you will never see a fat marathon runner?	• The teacher attempts to control the classroom. He addresses the comment and asks the question for a second time.
	Andre	Its basically because the be sweat'in	• Andre offers the first claim and link fat loss to sweat.
	Teacher	That's good. What does sweat have to do with it?	• The teacher validates his answer and asks for a more detailed description of the relationship between fat and sweat.
	Tanisha	It's because they always be hot. They be hotter than everybody else. My cousin always be sweat'in.	• Tanisha suggest heat plays a role in the process.
	Steve	"It's cause they fat Blood! (laughter). They get hot and they always be sweat'in . . . even if they just walk'in up the stairs."	• Steve attempts to validate Tanisha's answer.
	D'Andre	"Naw! It's like this. It's like if you set a block of ice out. Out on the curb. The ice don't just melt. First, it just turns into water. Then, the water it disappears into steam. It's like that. It don't be no fat marathon runners because when they run, they melt the fat and they body use the fat and it burns off."	• D'Andre disputes their claim by saying "Naw." He then offers a new explanation based on phase changes in fat by using an analogy.

Source: Adapted from Bryan Brown, "Isn't That Just Good Teaching? Disaggregate Instruction and the Language Identity Dilemma," *The Journal of Science Teacher Education* 22 (2011): 679–704.

CONCEPTUAL CONTINUITY—TWEAKING LINGUISTIC RELATIVISM

Years before writing this book, I conducted a two-year ethnographic study of such linguistic relativity. From 2006 to 2008, I served as an assistant coach for a local baseball team as a means to gain entry into the culture of the community. This study sought to understand what students knew about the science of a curveball, and to make sense of what language resources students used to represent their knowledge. The resulting analysis led me to reconceive the relationship between language, identity, and cognition.

If students' knowledge can be represented by multiple language types, then teachers must examine the multiple applications of what counts as science language. The idea is rooted in the nature of human inquiry. A framework from Charles Anderson and Ajay Sharma offers an explanation of how we generate science explanations through our experiences (see figure 3.1). As individuals move through the world, they have numerous experiences. These experiences produce a smaller number of patterns. As people begin to recognize these patterns, they

FIGURE 3.1   Anderson and Sharma's EPE Framework

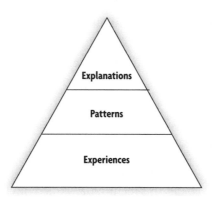

Source: Ajay Sharma and Charles Anderson, "Transforming Scientists' Science into School Science," paper delivered at the National Association for Research in Science Teaching, Philadelphia, March 23, 2003.

offer an even smaller number of explanations to make sense of their experiences.[5]

I would argue that we must now begin to consider the language that is used in those explanations. The language in which students use to express their science knowledge is rooted in the culture that grounds their experiences. If the explanations generated in one context are similar to and maintain continuity with scientific explanations in a classroom canonical genre, we must be able to recognize the conceptual continuity of those statements to the science concepts—that science concepts and their subcomponents can be explained using a variety of discourses. The example below provides a case of what becomes visible when we reason from a conceptual continuity perspective.

Learning About Baseball, Learning Physics

When learning to throw, successful baseball pitchers must learn to make the ball move by focusing on two critical movements. First, if they can produce a rapid vertical spin, a unique phenomenon occurs. The ball will be affected by differences in relative air pressure on either side. This is due to the relationship between the air and the seams of the baseball. On one side of the baseball, the seams will spin the direction of the airflow, while on the other side, the seams will go against the airflow, producing a greater air pressure on that side of the ball. This pressure differential, or Magnus Effect, will cause the ball to change directions rapidly, and the impact of Magnus forces will generate a rapid downward movement. In the baseball community, this is known as the *12-to-6 curveball*. This colloquial term uses a clock analogy to describe the directional velocity change that occurs. A second pitching technique is based on this same principle. This technique also takes advantage of the Magnus Effect, which causes the ball to move at an angle. Using this technique, skilled pitchers can cause the ball to move from right to left (for right-handed pitchers) and left to right (for left-handed pitchers). In baseball terminology, this is known as a *curveball* or *slider*.

Being able to throw these pitches does not require players to learn why they work the way they do. However, I was curious as to whether this community and its cultural resources included learning about why curveballs curved. I asked a basic question: "Please describe how the seams play a part in how the ball moves through the air when the pitcher attempts a curveball." What we discovered was a fascinating mixture of linguistic representations of students' knowledge.

The student-athletes used a variety of everyday discourse to describe the curveball phenomenon. By *everyday discourse*, I refer to the use of words and phrases not rooted in baseball or scientific discourses—words accessible to the general public, including words like *push*, *pull*, *air*, *wind*, *fast*, and *slow*.

We found students had unique ways of describing science concepts like air pressure, changes in velocity, directional terms, force, spin, and wind influence. For example, one student stated, "When you snap your wrist, it forces the ball to spin like this, and then air will continue to push it against the seams." The student recognized that air represents an agent of force. Another student explained "I don't know if it's high or low, but one of them is on the top and one of them is on the bottom—the top one's pushing it down in kind of an arc and the one on the bottom can't hold up to it."

What becomes interesting about these descriptions is the continuity they maintain with scientific explanations. In the first, the student explains how the air continues to "push against the seams." He clearly understands that the relationship between the seams and the air pushing the ball. But instead of explaining that there is greater "air pressure" due to this relationship, he describes it as a *push*. In the second example, the student explains how the top of the ball is being "pushed" down harder than on the bottom of the ball.

Again, he knows that the seams on the top of the ball cause the ball to change direction.

Because they were free to use everyday terms, student-athletes were able to skillfully explain a number of concepts. Let's look at another player's explanation of how air pressure impacts the movement of a curveball: "When you snap your wrist, it forces the ball to spin like *this [manually spins ball in air to demonstrate the spin]*, and the air will continue to push it against the seams." Again, the verb he uses is *push*. Although the scientific term *air pressure* is never used, this description maintains a great deal of continuity with the scientific alternative.

Another linguistic resource I identified in this process involved the unique ways student-athletes used the discourse of baseball to describe the movement of curveballs. We discovered that students were able to use the cognitive resources embedded in baseball language to differentiate between several concepts. For example, to describe relative changes in velocity, one student explains, "For a curve ball to work, you got to put a lot of rotation on it so it spins enough so it *breaks*, and it's not on a straight line." *Breaking* here refers to a quick directional change in velocity. A good curveball breaks, while a poorly thrown baseball will do the opposite, *hang*.

We found students made use of a wide diversity of terms and phrases to describe directional changes in the ball's movement that were all part of the discourse of baseball—*falling off the table*, *bite*, *hanging*, *diving*, *12-to-6*, *two-point curve* and *slurve* were all used to describe the differences in the directional changes of curveballs. A ball that *falls off the table* is the ideal curveball, one that that experiences a dramatic change in velocity where the ball drops rapidly. *Diving* was also used in this same context. The terms *12-to-6* and *two-point* described vertical changes in directional velocity. *Slurve* and *knee bender* described pitches whose changes in directional velocity were diagonal. Ultimately, what became clear, as students expressed knowledge through baseball language, was that their knowledge was represented by a dynamic vocabulary that would not be part of their classroom lexicon.

What emerged as most interesting for us in this study was these student-athletes' ability to differentiate between ideas using only the language of baseball. But ideas that were clear for students might be confusing if a conceptual continuity lens was not applied. Some terms used uniformly by the players had meanings very different than their use in a science context. When players would say a ball had *movement*, they intended to express that the ball moved rapidly and changed directional velocity. A ball that travels straight is easier to hit than one that suddenly changes directions; as a result, players attempted to make the ball change directional velocity, or "move" it. On the other hand, the term *velocity*, as used by the players, meant that a ball moved fast. This baseball meaning was nearly the opposite of the science meaning.

This finding demonstrated how students' complex knowledge was rooted in the language of their learning environment: baseball. Without a lens that recognized the linguistic relativity and continuity between ideas, these baseball players' knowledge of the science behind the behavior of different pitches would be difficult to understand.

I propose that scholars and educators operate from a position that values the conceptual continuities that exist across language types. There are two sorts of continuities between everyday language types and scientific language types. There are conceptual continuities that are purely linguistic. These continuities emerge when words in one context are synonymous with a scientific alternative. If students use *grippiness* as a synonym for *friction,* there is a linguistic conceptual continuity between terms. Table 3.2 shows how I derived this understanding by noting how the language of baseball produced several of these linguistic conceptual continuities. In that case, the words *movement* and *velocity* had synonyms in science language: *velocity* and *speed*. If one does not operate from a conceptual continuity lens, the actual meanings of these terms would be left misunderstood.

A second type of continuity is of a *conceptual* nature—when words, phrases, and metaphors share conceptual meanings with scientific terms. In these cases, the language that students use would describe analogical and compartmental understanding of concepts that are not expressed in science language. That is, students offer expressions of concepts that are all correct except for the words. These more challenging conceptions of phenomena require teachers to look closely at the phrases, terms, and examples students use to express their understanding with an assumption that their knowledge lives well beyond the words alone. We encountered this type of continuity in the dynamic ways students in the baseball study used the spin-to-speed relationship to explain why curveballs curve and accurately explained how the seams produced the air pressure responsible for a curveball's movement (see table 3.2).

LANGUAGE, RACE, AND WELL BEYOND

The ultimate point of this chapter is to highlight how our conceptions of language, race, and cognition hinder our ability to hear what students know. Students bring a wealth of knowledge with them as they enter learning environments, but our understanding of the relative value of their language resources is critical to how we will serve them. Luis Moll and his colleagues provide the research community with the language to describe this, using the phrase *funds of knowledge* to explain the conceptual and cultural resources students bring with them to the classroom.[6] This discussion of conceptual continuity intends to add to that literature by demonstrating how students' linguistic resources must be considered for their cognitive value.

TABLE 3.2   Types of conceptual continuity

Baseball language	Definition	Science language	Parallel meaning
Linguistic Conceptual Continuities			
Baseball movement	Student-athletes described the rapid movement or change in the direction of the ball as it approaches the hitter.	The scientific word *velocity* offers a description of the dramatic change in the direction of an any moving object.	The student-athletes in this scenario do not use the scientific term but have an alternative that makes the distinction between simple speed and the rate in which an object changes direction.
Baseball velocity	Student-athletes regularly used the word velocity to identify the speed of the ball as it approaches the plate.	The scientific term speed identifies the rate an object travels across a given distance.	In baseball student-athletes use velocity to make the distinction between how fast the baseball travels directly and how rapidly it moves in different directions as it approaches the batter.
Baseball language	Definition	Science language	Parallel meaning
Cognitive Conceptual Continuities			
Relationship between spin and speed	Student-athletes offered explanations for the reasoning for a curveball's movement by identifying the role of the relationship between the spin of the ball and its speed.	The Magnus forces describe how differential forces due to air pressure produce a curveball's movement.	Student-athletes describe a similar pattern of forces that impact the ball's trajectory. They identify the key pressure points that influence the ball.
Air and resistance and interaction with seams	The student-athletes described the key role of the seams and air as the key factor to forcing the downward movement of the baseball.	The raised seams of a baseball are key in altering the trajectory of the baseball. When spun rapidly, seams will push against the passing air to produce a differential air pressure effect.	Without using science language, student athletes describe the impact of the seams on the aerodynamics of the ball.

Source: Adapted from Bryan Brown and Matthew Kloser, "Conceptual Continuity and Accessing Everyday Scientific Understandings," *Cultural Studies in Science Education* 4 (2009): 875–897.

What is central to this perspective is altering our assumptions about what we believe students know. When we switch from a lens that views the culture of urban students as deficient and lacking nuance to one that values the cognitive resources embedded in students' modes of communicating, we may no longer be surprised by what our students have to offer.

In some ways, we teach students under false pretenses. We celebrate them when they use science language accurately, but we never establish a framework for how science language should be learned. In a generation with more multilingual and multicultural students than ever in the classroom, teachers will have to broaden their conception of science language. Science language involves a beautiful mix of terms used in contexts well beyond the classroom. If we want access to what students truly know, we must measure students on what we teach and learn to understand the beauty of what they already know.

CHAPTER 4

More Than an Apple That Day

A Simple Matter of Learning

MY STUDIES OF HOW language and cognition are connected emerged from my interactions with children. I am no Piaget—I never use my children as a micro-laboratory to understand learning—but any parent knows that our theories of learning are truly tested when we are entrenched in our most difficult teaching job: the teaching of our own children.

Like many parents, I was amazed at the rapid language development of my son. He would hear new words and quickly use them in as many situations as he could, as if his one-year-old mind understood its own capacity to learn. There was an aggressive acquisition of words as his mother and I attempted to talk to him as if he were a five-year-old child.

I vividly remember the day he changed my mind about how language and learning are connected. We were together in the kitchen, and he was standing at the counter looking at a green apple on the countertop. He began to whine and point at the apple. At this time, he was close to two years old, so a whine as a request for food was inadequate, in my eyes. Instead of simply giving the apple to him, I asked him to use his words. To my surprise, as clear as day, he pointed and said "Apple, please."

These words are not that impressive, but rather could be expected from a child of that age. For me, the insight was simultaneously profound and simple. He knew the word *apple* but *chose* not to use it. If I had merely handed him the apple, I doubt that he would have actually used the word. This process was fascinating to me. My asking him to use the word generated an opportunity for him to use that word in the appropriate context. This was only valuable if he knew the word first and was then required to use it in a meaningful way.

If he did not know the word, the question would not have been *generative*—a word I use to express the idea that teachers have the opportunity to produce experiences that *generate* clarity and cognitive schema for their students. These opportunities to explain allow students to gain an understanding of their ideas. In this case, forcing my son to say the word *apple* produced an opportunity for him to affirm his understanding that the word was the appropriate one and that it produced the appropriate result. Additionally, he had to know what an apple was in order for the word to have value in his one-year-old world. I had read about situated cognition, constructivism, and psychologist Lev Vygotsky's *Thought and Language,* but this simple interaction merged those ideas for me in a meaningful way.[1]

THE APPLE IN SITUATED COGNITION

The idea that served as the principal explanation of this story is *situated cognition*—the theory that our knowledge is deeply connected to the situations and meaningful contexts where people learn.[2] We learn in situations that require us to gain knowledge. As a result, we understand that learning never happens in a vacuum, but rather it occurs in the situations where knowing means the most to the learner. Research on situated cognition explains how students construct knowledge in environments that require learning to happen.[3]

The critical dimensions of people's daily activity define the constraints of their learning; that is, learning is deeply situational and embedded in activities. For example, as a carpenter prepares to make a chair, the task of measurement becomes a vital aspect of the experience. A common saying among carpenters, "Measure twice, cut once," drives home the importance of this task: accuracy is so critical to the experience that a carpenter should be very sure that the measurements are correct before making an irreversible, inaccurate cut and having to start again. Being a carpenter requires learning about measurement in an authentic way. This is the situated cognition position.

In a landmark article exploring situated cognition and the culture of learning, John Seely Brown and colleagues offer a nuanced explanation of how learning is deeply embedded in the situations that drive our daily lives: "All knowledge is, we believe, like language. Its constituent parts index the world and so are inextricably a product of the activity and situations in which they are produced. A concept, for example, will continually evolve with each new occasion of use, because new situations, negotiations, and activities inevitably recast is in a new, more densely textured form. So a concept, like the meaning of a word, is always under construction."[4]

This description explains the apple story. The situation that my son was in, where he could not grab the apple himself, produced an opportunity for him to use his limited language skills. His initial whining was met with a request for a word that I did not provide him. Ultimately, his asking for an apple was a product of the situation he was in. He knew the word, he was in a situation where the word was useful to him, and he was asked to use the word in a meaningful way.

To me, this exchange offered an analogy for how teaching and learning should happen in science. As young people are introduced to new ideas, we have to craft authentic experiences that require them to use their new ideas in critically important ways. As teachers, we have to skillfully produce activities where students have to create and offer explanations using science language. By doing so, these situations will drive students to use science language and ultimately learn the ideas and language being taught.

CONSTRUCTIVISM AS LEARNING ABOUT "APPLE"

A second understanding that emerged from this experience was a better appreciation of *socioconstructivism*, the idea that students make sense of thing by using the resources of their environment grew stronger after reflecting on this exchange. As we interact with the resources in the world we live in, we constantly shape, revise, and revisit the ideas that make up our immediate world.

On that day, my son learned something about apples and words. When he was asked to "use your words," he was given access to an expectation of language. Simultaneously, he was being made aware that asking for an apple by name was a valued activity in our household. Unfortunately, our exchange about the apple ended there, so I cannot recount how he used the word *apple* moving forward. What I can say is that I learned that requiring learners to use language in meaningful ways produced an opportunity to appropriate new language.

In today's educational environment, teachers and scholars enthusiastically adhere to constructivist teaching environments where young people work together to make meaning of the concepts they are learning. Compared with traditional instructional monologues, carefully constructed learning tasks produce numerous opportunities for student learning. However, we must question the extent to which these activities are actually generative. Having students in groups provides opportunities for discussion, but are these discussions producing learning? To what extent do teaching practices generate opportunities for students to learn both the content and the language used to represent those ideas? The teacher as the expert participant in discussion must create opportunities for students to "use their words" if they are ever to become able to appropriate the science discourse.

In reflecting on the story of the apple and the countertop, I began to reconsider psychologist Lev Vygotsky's position on *inner* and *outer speech*—the idea that words are different than the discourse in our mind. Pressley and McCormick explain the division in this way: "In particular, inner speech is abbreviated and fragmentary, with the meaning of complex thoughts captured in few words."[5] This means that thoughts are represented by words, but these representations are not linear and may not hold a simple one-to-one parallel relationship. In fact, Vygotsky's landmark text on language and cognition, *Thought and Language*, makes the case that we have the cognitive capability to cluster things in meaningful representations and that when we think, we see pictures of things that are dynamic and multimodal. Because we have this ability, these pictures in our minds are more like movies with representations existing in clusters of moving parts that together hold specific meaning. The idea that is most central here is that these mental representations are not simply words. According to Vygotsky, "Thought does not consist of individual words like speech. I may want to express the thought that I saw a barefoot boy in a blue shirt running down the street today. I do not, however, see separately the boy, the shirt, the fact that the shirt was blue, the fact that the boy ran, and the fact that the boy was without shoes. I see all of this together in a unified act of thought."[6] This powerful representation highlights how understanding exists separate from the words. It also highlights that thoughts exist in ways that words simply lack the capacity to match.

DISAGGREGATE INSTRUCTION

To think that understanding what an apple is, knowing its label (i.e., word), and choosing to use the word to request it are all unique actions and all components of learning was new territory for me. Considering the dynamic relationship between language, cognition, and learning led me to question why contemporary teaching ignored this relationship and chose not to address each component separately. In the end, this reflection caused me to explore the possibilities of teaching science as both concept learning and as language learning in a process known as *disaggregate instruction.*

Disaggregating the relationship between thought and language seemed revolutionary to me. It suggested that effective teaching should mirror the process of efficient learning—thinking about how we can use language to represent ideas and how our instruction should take time to teach students the language of science as well. I grew convinced that our ability to understand ideas is deeply connected to the types of mental representations we could ultimately make available to students. The assumption was that once mental representations were clear, then learning the language associated with the concept would become easier; that is, the students would be better able to learn that language.

Although disaggregate instruction is about improving academic language learning, mastering the language of science is different than merely learning a new language in several critical ways. First, learning the language of science is a cognitive task that is more complicated than learning a new language alone. When we learn a new language, we are learning new words for ideas we already know. By contrast, learning the language of science requires the student to simultaneously learn new words and new ideas. However, exploring the relationship between language, cognition, and learning is critical to reducing the complication embedded in learning the academic language of science. Second, the language of science has a number of alternative and colloquial terms that have multiple meanings in students' lives. For example, the term *force* can be used to influencing a person to do something, not *mass × acceleration*. Third, students may have conceptual understanding that does not rely on scientific terminology. As I noted in chapter 3, students may hold nuanced conceptual understandings that are represented in everyday language practices. Finally, science language involves multiple representations including new words, new graphical depictions, new symbol systems, and mathematical representations of science concepts. For example, a simple lesson on meiosis in biology may include mathematical probability and new words like *chromatid*, *chromatin*, and *chromosomes*, as well as the need to understand microscopic images of genes in haploid and diploid form.

To explore this issue, I decided to study what would happen if the focus on teaching shifted toward a model that valued disaggregating instruction. In 2004, I proposed using a disaggregate approach to teaching as a way to reduce the language identity conflict in science.[7] I reasoned that if teachers clearly articulated the language expectations of the class, then students would be less likely to be negatively characterized by their use of science language. If everyone were required to use science language, then everyone would experience the same cultural expectations as opposed to allowing the use of science language to become the property of one racial group. A second potential benefit to learning this way was that introducing the concept in simple language would help the students gain a clear understanding of the basics of the content. This would allow the students to learn the academic language associated with the content more efficiently.

DISAGGREGATE INSTRUCTION PEDAGOGY

Disaggregate instruction is a four-stage teaching process that includes pre-assessment, everyday content construction, explicit language instruction, and scaffolding opportunities for discourse. These stages are designed to make the initial concept clear, while ensuring students gain a mastery of the academic language.

Phase One: Pre-Assessment

Instruction should start with a pre-assessment of the students' understanding of the concept. This assessment can be a written embedded assessment or an oral pre-assessment. Discovering what students know about the concept provides the teacher with two critical resources. First, instead of operating from a dichotomous "right-or-wrong" perspective, the teacher will be able to start instruction with a clear vision of what aspects of the subject the students seem to be clear about. Second, the teacher can identify what language resources students bring with them. Understanding what words students use to describe the concept allows the teacher to consider what linguistic resources are available to them that can potentially be used to introduce the idea.

For example, in an attempt to teach fifth graders photosynthesis (part of an experiment conducted with my former graduate student and current professor of science education, Kihyun Ryoo), the pre-assessment led to an interesting language discovery. Students were describing carbon dioxide as the "bad air" that humans breathe out and were describing oxygen as the "good air" that humans breathe in, which turned out to be a good way to represent the basic idea of each gas. Although humans breathe out other gases in addition to carbon dioxide, using those phrases introduced the idea that students could build a clear conception of these gases. As long as we added the appropriate terminology later, these language resources helped us improve students' initial understanding of the concept of photosynthesis.

Phase Two: Everyday Content Construction

The second aspect of disaggregated instruction involves *everyday content instruction*. The idea is to offer the big idea or fundamental premise of instruction using everyday, accessible language. After completing a pre-assessment, a teacher should have information about what linguistic resources students have to make the concept clear. The goal of the content construction phase is to engage students in instructional activities that make the big idea of the concept available to them without introducing the complex science discourse.

For example, for the lesson on photosynthesis, our pre-assessment yielded valuable information. We learned that students used unique phrases to distinguish between types of air. Using the phrases *the bad air that humans breathe out* and *the good air that humans breathe in*, they had linguistic resources that would help build understanding of the idea. As we design activities for the content construction phase, we use this critical information. We might start with a mini-lecture that tells the story of how the leaves of plants use our "bad air" and convert it into "good air." We can have students build a model of the "energy pouches" (an accessible term to introduce the concept of chloroplasts) that use a combination of "bad air" and sunlight to create "good air" and sugar. This can be accompanied with a microscope activity where students can view magnified chloroplasts. The goal is to make the big idea as clear and accessible as possible prior to introducing the new science language.

Phase Three: Explicit Language Instruction

In the *explicit language instruction* phase, the teacher structures activities to teach the students the new science language. After students explore the fundamentals of the ideas with simple terms like *good air*, *bad air*, and *energy pouches*, the terms are paired with their scientific synonyms. The concept behind this is that adding a new label for an concept that is understood is more efficient than attempting to teach the label and the concept simultaneously. The teacher must then structure activities where students are taught that the "energy pouch" is called a *chloroplast*, the "bad air" that is released is known as *carbon dioxide*, and the "good air" is known as *oxygen*.

These activities can be diverse and creative. One can image a teacher merely offering a two- to three-minute lecture to explain what the new terms are. Alternatively, a teacher can ask students to use texts to substitute the scientific term for the everyday term. Over the years, I have seen my students create fictitious social media (e.g., Facebook, MySpace, Twitter) pages for this purpose. In these instances, teachers created printouts of the Facebook page for photosynthesis. Students were asked to label the parts and actions of the photosynthesis image by replacing the everyday terms with more appropriate scientific terms.

Ultimately, the point is to make students aware that language mastery is a component of their learning task. Unlike allowing academic language learning to be a subtext of instruction, this phase is designed to make language learning an explicit aspect of the students' instructional experience.

Phase Four: Scaffolding Opportunities for Discourse

The final phase of instruction involves the scaffolding of opportunities to learn the science discourse. If the pathway to true academic fluency is having opportunities to explain the phenomena being studied, the instruction should be based on this premise. Therefore, in this phase teachers create opportunities for students to explain the concept but require them to use their new science terminology. This aspect of pedagogy is built on the assumption that if students are to become clear about the details of a topic being taught, we must give them several opportunities to explain the concept and must require them to practice their science language.

For instance, to continue with the photosynthesis example, a formative assessment activity can be designed to provide students an opportunity for mastery. A teacher might design an exercise where students are asked the following:

A group of foresters are planning on cutting down the Redwood Forest. They want to sell the wood. People are mad because they say we need the trees and they need us. CBS news spots you on the street and asks your opinion. What would you say? In your answer use the following words (*chloroplasts, photons, oxygen, carbon dioxide, glucose*). Use the space below to write, and be prepared to share with a partner.

This sample formative assessment task is designed to generate learning opportunities. Engaging in this task is akin to being asked to "use your words." The intent is to provide students with an opportunity to use their new science language in meaningful ways prior to their summative assessment. This stands in stark contrast to educators' common bad habit of not allowing students opportunities to express their understanding until the final assessment. This small addition of requiring them to use their new science terms ensures that students are provided the opportunity to appropriate science language.

Collectively, these four stages reflect an adoption of constructivist and situated cognition perspectives on learning. In using students' everyday language resources and separating the basic ideas from the language, I am hoping students can pair their cognition and words in a way that reflects Vygotsky's assumptions of their relationship. By scaffolding students' use of new discourse through formative assessment, this approach situates language learning in a manner that reflects a *cognitive apprenticeship framework* on learning. Together, these subtle changes to teacher planning have the potential to positively impact the language cognition relationship for students.

DOES DISAGGREGATE INSTRUCTION WORK? AN EXPERIMENT

Disaggregate instruction pedagogy was the logical result of theoretical considerations. However, life in urban schools is far more than apples on countertops. To examine whether this type of pedagogy would actually work, I decided to conduct an experiment. Working collaboratively, Kihyun Ryoo and I designed a small-scale experiment to test how disaggregate instruction would compare to an alternative.[8]

Initially, we hoped to conduct a simple classroom experiment with multiple teachers teaching in an experimental and controlled way. However, we were concerned that the impact of the teacher's skill would influence the outcome. We were also concerned that the teachers might apply the method differently. Additionally, the number of teachers necessary for conducting this experiment was intimidating. There were simply too many moving parts to trust in teacher training and application. As an alternative, we chose to conduct a computer-based experiment in which we could carefully control the type of pedagogy students experienced. In choosing to use a computer as instructor, we could ensure that every student was taught in exactly the same way. This controlled experimental environment helped us reduce the number of variables that might impact the overall quality of the experiment.

Design

To measure the potential effectiveness of disaggregate instruction, we took care to design an experiment that isolated language. For our controlled condition, we decided to teach new ideas and new language simultaneously, while in the experimental condition, we used the disaggregate approach to teach the concept first and language second. Figure 4.1 provides an overview of the primary design of our research. To provide us with a baseline measure of relative performance between the groups, we gave each group a pre-test that comprised eighteen questions about photosynthesis. Each group was given a different type of instruction (experimental or controlled) and was then given the post-assessment. That post-assessment was also an eighteen-item assessment of their knowledge of photosynthesis.

FIGURE 4.1   Design of the research

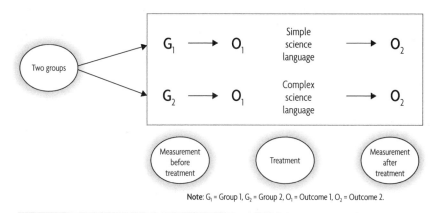

Note: G_1 = Group 1, G_2 = Group 2, O_1 = Outcome 1, O_2 = Outcome 2.

Equitable Conditions

To make sure we were able to focus on the difference in teaching and not differences in other features, we were attentive to making the conditions of teaching equitable. To do this, we made all the images used for instruction exactly the same. The only thing that differed was the language used to introduce the idea. Figure 4.2 provides an example of how we introduced the concept of photosynthesis in the experimental condition. In this instance, we used words we discovered in pre-assessment to introduce photosynthesis. The phrases "good air that all living things need for breathing" and "air that humans breathe out" were used as replacements for their more scientific synonyms.

Figure 4.3 pictures the control group version of the same image. The image is identical to that shown in figure 4.2, but we replaced the everyday terms with scientific terms.

In a further attempt to keep the conditions equitable, we used the same process to introduce other ideas. In the control condition, the chloroplast is shown with scientific labels of the carbon dioxide and photons entering the thykaloid membranes (see figure 4.4). In the experimental group, we used terms like *green pigment* and *energy pouch*

FIGURE 4.2 Sample of the experimental condition

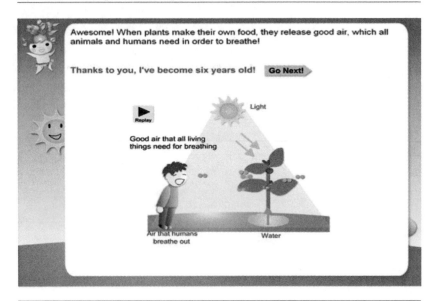

FIGURE 4.3 Sample of the control condition

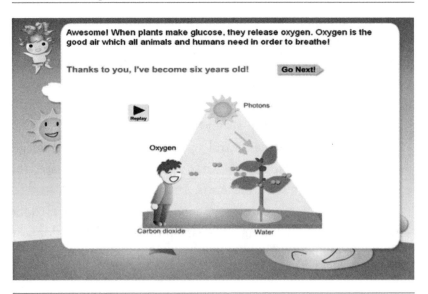

FIGURE 4.4   Sample of science language introductions

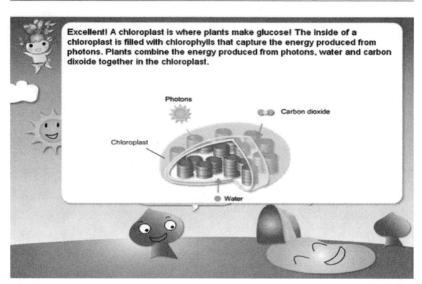

Excellent! A chloroplast is where plants make glucose! The inside of a chloroplast is filled with chlorophylls that capture the energy produced from photons. Plants combine the energy produced from photons, water and carbon dixoide together in the chloroplast.

Photons

Carbon dioxide

Chloroplast

Water

to create an everyday language alternative (see figure 4.5). Overall, we used the computer software as a way to standardize the time of instruction and the way students received information.

To measure students' relative learning gains, we used a pre- and post-test design with three types of measure:

1. *Disaggregate questions*: These questions were asked using the same everyday language used in the instruction. We did this to determine if the effect was due to the language used to ask the question or to the students' content knowledge.

2. *Aggregate questions*: These were questions asked using traditional science language.

3. *Overall scores*: The final assessment included the students' performance on both of the question types as well as a summary of their performance on multiple-choice questions and written short-answer questions.

FIGURE 4.5   Sample of simple language introductions

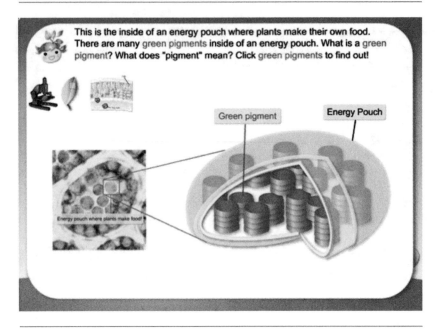

Working in conjunction with an elementary school in a large northern California city, we conducted our experiment with fifty students from two classrooms.

Findings

Upon analyzing the completed assessments, we found that students taught using the disaggregate approach showed greater learning gains on all three measures. Although both groups improved their total scores in the post-test, the experimental group improved at a faster rate. Their improvement was statistically significant and suggested that altering how language is introduced has the potential to impact students' learning. Table 4.1 shows how the experimental group's overall score increased by 23.42 percent, while the control group's

TABLE 4.1 Learning results of the experiment

	Achievement (max)	Group	n	Pre-test score (SD)	Post-test score (SD)	Raw gain	%	t	Effect size
No.	**A**	**B**	**C**	**D**	**E**	**F**	**G**	**H**	**I**
1	Overall score (76)	Treatment	25	11.60 (5.56)	29.40 (12.73)	17.80	+23.42	8.70**	1.74
		Control	24	10.79 (5.31)	19.29 (8.89)	8.50	+11.18	4.72**	0.96
2	Disaggregate score (39)	Treatment	25	6.76 (3.60)	17.80 (6.58)	11.04	+28.31	9.35**	1.86
		Control	24	6.58 (3.24)	11.17 (4.87)	4.59	+11.77	4.35**	0.89
3	Aggregate score (37)	Treatment	25	4.84 (2.61)	11.60 (6.47)	6.76	+18.27	6.70**	1.34
		Control	24	4.21 (2.38)	8.13 (4.27)	3.92	+10.59	4.64**	0.95

p > 0.001 = **

Source: Adapted from Bryan Brown and Kihyun Ryoo, "Teaching Science as a Language: A 'Content-First' Approach to Science Teaching," *The Journal of Research in Science Teaching* 45 (2008): 525–664. © NARST: A Worldwide Organization for Improving Science Teaching and Learning Through Research.

overall scored increased at a rate of 11.18 percent. These findings verified our assumption that teaching in a disaggregate fashion could improve students' learning.

A simple reflection on the mean scores of both groups before and after treatment demonstrates this effect. Prior to teaching, the control group mean of 10.79 was just 0.81 points lower than the experimental group. This suggests that as a whole, the experimental group was slightly stronger than the control group prior to the experiment. After receiving the disaggregate instruction approach, the experimental group's mean score of 29.40 was 10.11 points higher than the treatment group's mean score of 19.29. If we consider that the control group experienced a mean gain of 17.80 points while the control group experienced a mean gain of 8.5 points, we can see just how powerful an effect this small alteration in language had on students' cognition.

SIMPLE VERSUS COMPLEX LANGUAGE

To make sure our results were not merely a result of the way we asked our questions, we analyzed how each group scored on questions written in scientific language and in simple everyday language. Figure 4.6 presents students' scores on each question type. The pattern was consistent in the percentage of correct answers on both disaggregate (everyday language) and aggregate (scientific language) questions. What emerged as interesting in this analysis was how the results of the scientific questions were lower for both groups. This suggests that learning to master the language is a difficult task regardless of the approach. Despite this, we discovered that the students in the experimental group performed much better than their counterparts in the control group (see figure 4.7).

In our final step in assessing the differences in students' learning, we separated our analysis of the multiple-choice questions and the short written questions. We were interested in measuring the impact of disaggregate teaching on the students' ability to select the answer compared with their ability to produce their own cogent explanation. In analyzing these results, we found our most powerful outcomes. Table 4.2 compares the results across assessment types, demonstrating

FIGURE 4.6   Learning results by question type

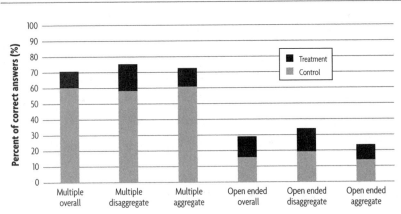

Source: Bryan Brown and Kihyun Ryoo, "Teaching Science as a Language: A 'Content-First' Approach to Science Teaching," *The Journal of Research in Science Teaching* 45 (May 2008): 529–553. © NARST: A Worldwide Organization for Improving Science Teaching and Learning Through Research.

FIGURE 4.7   Comparisons of learning goals by group

Source: Adapted from Bryan Brown and Kihyun Ryoo, "Teaching Science as a Language: A 'Content-First' Approach to Science Teaching." *The Journal of Research in Science Teaching* 45 (2018): 525–664. © NARST: A Worldwide Organization for Improving Science Teaching and Learning Through Research.

TABLE 4.2   Comparison of learning gains by group

No.	Achievement	Max	Group	n	Mean	SD	p	t	Effect size
	A		B	C	D	E	F	H	I
				Multiple choice questions					
1	Overall score	18	Treatment	25	12.48	3.47	0.046	2.05*	0.59
			Control	24	10.38	3.72			
2	Disaggregate score	10	Treatment	25	7.40	2.10	0.010	2.67*	0.76
			Control	24	5.71	2.33			
3	Aggregate score	8	Treatment	25	5.08	1.87	0.433	0.79	0.22
			Control	24	4.67	1.79			
				Open-ended question					
4	Overall score	58	Treatment	25	16.92	9.89	0.001	3.384**	0.97
			Control	24	8.92	6.16			
5	Disaggregate score	29	Treatment	25	10.40	5.11	0.000	3.987***	1.14
			Control	24	5.46	3.34			
6	Aggregate score	29	Treatment	25	6.52	4.93	0.012	2.616*	0.75
			Control	24	3.46	2.98			

* = p < 0.05, ** = p < 0.01, *** = p < 0.001

that the differences in the performances of the groups were statistically significant across all measures (see table 4.2). The mean score for post-test results for written items was 16.92 for the experimental group compared to 8.92 for the control group. These results suggest that the treatment group was nearly twice as strong in their retention. As seen in figure 4.6, the trend that emerged highlights that the difference between the groups grew on short-answer items and closed on multiple-choice questions. This suggests that after instruction, the biggest difference in the groups' performance was seen in their ability to explain what they knew without prompting.

To measure the impact of this intervention, we also conducted effect size assessments to measure the extent to which our treatment was responsible for movements in the standard deviation of the participating groups. As seen in table 4.2, we found moderate effect sizes of 0.59 for the multiple-choice questions overall. In particular, the strong effect size of 0.76 for disaggregate questions suggests that when questions were asked with simple language, the control group performed better. The effect size of 0.22 suggests that when scientific language multiple-choice questions were asked, there was little effect.

Where this data becomes intriguing is in the manner in which writing answers was strongly impacted. As seen in table 4.2, when students were asked to write their own answers, there was a strong effect size of 0.97. This was particularly strong when students were asked about the content in simple language (disaggregate score). In these instances, there was an incredibly strong effect size of 1.14. In perhaps our most interesting results, we found an effect size of 0.75 for questions asked in science language. In these instances, students who were taught in everyday language mastered the capacity to write and explain in science language even when they were not taught in that language initially. Simply said, those taught with simple language were better able to answer complex science language questions than their counterparts.

Ultimately, the students who were taught phenomena in everyday terms demonstrated superior learning gains regardless of the types of questions used to assess their understanding. Given the almost identical pre-test mean scores for both groups, the greater gain of the treatment group's post score speaks volumes regarding the impact of the content-first approach.

A RETURN TO THE APPLE STORY

I learned a lot from that apple incident. Teachers are faced with numerous challenges, and helping their students master academic language should be included as a priority. To do this, we need to develop a clearer understanding of how language and learning work. More importantly, teachers must meet the language-learning need with the instruction best suited to their students. I don't claim that disaggregate instruction is the sole or best way to approach this challenge. Rather, I hope to encourage scholars and teachers to explore ways we can meaningfully improve the academic language learning. When we take a language-focused approach and require students to use their words, we can truly maximize students' potential.

CHAPTER 5

The Verbal Advantage

Sounding Smart and Feeling Good?

AS A YOUNG PROFESSOR, my desire to work in urban communities changed my lifestyle: it made me a commuter. As I endured the cacophony of traffic with my thoughts wandering from ideas about work to thoughts about the mundane tasks of family life, I would often dissect radio commercials. I relished especially badly designed commercials chuckling over a radio voice attempting to sound like a "trusted lawyer" or like a "sexy salesperson." But much of my dissection involved questions about the language of the ads themselves. I would ask "Who is this ad designed for?" "What fool thought this was the best way to market a product?" This exercise, though offering distraction, was rarely fruitful until the day I encountered an ad by a company called Verbal Advantage.

Verbal Advantage focuses on helping people develop an advanced vocabulary on the premise that people with complex vocabularies are smarter and more sophisticated. The website, which I subsequently looked up, states: "Fair or not, people make assumptions about your intelligence, your education and your capabilities by the words you use. Studies prove that a strong command of the English language is directly linked to career advancement, earnings and social success. To move ahead in your career, your vocabulary level must at least equal the average level of members of your profession."[1]

Imagine the joy I felt as my mundane ad dissection turned into an audio playground for a scholar interested in language and identity. I had my doubts about the value of the product, but I was fully aligned with its claims about how language worked. The idea that "people make assumptions about your intelligence" resonated with me, especially given the fact that I was in the process of writing about how language and identity are negotiated when people hear and speak to each other. If I agreed with nothing else on the air or on the site, I agreed with the fundamental assumption that there is something about the initial interpretation of how people speak that gives us information about who they are and how intelligent we anticipate they will be. Sometimes this initial perception is confirmed, and sometimes we find ourselves utterly disappointed with the statements we hear from someone we anticipated to be "intelligent."

In our moment-to-moment interactions, people judge us by the words we use, how we use them, and what we say with them. Those who are aware of this advantage are able to benefit from it, while others must suffer the subtle injustice of linguistic prejudice. The Verbal Advantage Company knew this to be the way of the world and sought to profit from it.

The positive attributes of this language-identity dimension became evident to me in graduate school. A well-meaning colleague who had developed a scholarly curiosity about African American intellectuals asked me a question that walked the fine line between insightful and racist: "Why do all the African American public intellectuals speak in such a hyper-academic way?" When I asked him for more details, he mentioned Cornel West, Michael Eric Dyson, and Tony Brown as examples.

For years, I considered his question. Could Michael Eric Dyson have ascended to his position in the pre-blogosphere public intellectual space without his trademark wordplay? Could Cornel West become the voice and icon for black intellectual life without his mastery of academic pontification? To me, these questions were secondary to the fact that these people were effective. Somehow, they were so effective in their communication of ideas that they avoided caricature and gave my curiosity-filled colleague an image of what African American intellectuals could be. For him, their approach to discourse produced a new association of black intellectuals with a complex and elegant use of the English language. Never mind that both men were theology professors who earned their intellectual chops in the church world. Their public use of discourse earned them a verbal advantage that caused my colleague to question whether or not this was a black intellectual thing.

As my car crawled across the bridge among slow moving commuters, I reflected on how identity mattered when we communicated ideas to others. There was something effective that Verbal Advantage bet its business model on—that there is a feeling that is a subtext to our communication. What they fail to mention is that race, culture, and aesthetic set the stage for what you feel and expect. Language is a marker of who we predict people to be. As a result, any advantage earned is earned in the face of what we know about how language works. So, if people earn a "verbal advantage," they must earn that advantage with the expectations of what people like them "should" sound like. Crossing the bridge on that day confirmed the idea that a person's language and identity signaled subtle cues about sounding smart.

DISCURSIVE IDENTITY: THE POTENTIAL VERBAL DISADVANTAGE

In thinking about how language allows people to take a particular position, I deeply considered how language and identity are connected.

People constantly frame each other by type. An individual can be labeled as *smart, goofy*, or any number of other dynamic qualifiers. Ultimately, an identity allows us to answer our questions of *who* a person is supposed to be. We make decisions about who we are and who the person is we are talking to.

So, how does this apply in the teaching and learning of science? The answer is obvious for those who teach in contexts where language tells the story of who you are. It affords a window through which we better perceive who has verbal advantages and disadvantages. In Los Angeles, Crips and Bloods play a constant language game. When someone asks you to pass the "bup" or tells you the party is going to be "bracking," they are sending you dual messages. They are asking you to hand them a cup and telling you that the party will be "cracking" (slang for *good*). But their strategic exchange of the letter *c* for the letter *b* is simultaneously informing you they are Bloods, as their affiliation with the Blood gang is marked by their deliberate use of language. Crips also use this practice. Young men may ask "What it C like?" instead of "What it be like?" or simply referring to everyone as "cuz." The consistent use of words starting with the letter *c* informs you that you are talking to a member of the Crip gang. Given this reality, asking kids to talk about *protons, ribosomal DNA, endoplasmic reticulum*, and *chromosome* may lead to some discomfort. How do students who are hypersensitive to what language says about who they are deal with the broad vocabulary and the complexity of academic language in science? Are teachers aware of this language interaction, and if so, what do they do about it? In this way, the verbal advantage and disadvantage of how language is used in the science classroom is deeply rooted in how students see themselves and how teachers ease this tension.

This subtext of language and identity serves as the foundation of the *language-identity dilemma*. The premise is that students—urban students in particular—often find themselves involved in complicated situations where what they know and what they learn are hindered by educators who simply ignore the relationship between language and identity.

LANGUAGE-IDENTITY DILEMMA

The *language-identity dilemma* is the idea that learning to master the language of an academic discipline, particularly science, presents a twofold challenge for students—a cognitive dilemma and an affective dilemma. In the cognitive sense, words represent ideas. As such, words can mean more than one thing, and a single idea can be encompassed by multiple words. For example, having a lot of "pressure" can mean experiencing a great deal of expectations. Alternatively, "pressure" can also refer to the amount of gas contained within a confined spaced. What if someone suggests that air is "smooshed" into a small jar? Are they referring to pressure? This is the cognitive challenge that emerges when we do not prepare teachers to make nuanced distinctions between the use of the word and whether or not a student understands the ideas.

When we add a layer of cultural identity to this cognitive analysis, we discover that people of certain cultures are more likely to use particular terms. If you ask a person in a neighborhood similar to the one I grew up in to explain how to throw a football further they might offer "Blood, you gotta use your hips to launch your hands and elbow. When you let it go spin it hard with your thumb and index finger, cause the harder it spins the air can't slow it down or push it either direction." This explanation does not use terms like *torque*, *velocity*, or *air resistance*. However, those *concepts* are being used in the explanation. We just need the ears to hear it. In contrast, imagine this same person in a science class whose teacher explains, "Throwing footballs accurately relies on applying the maximum torque and thrust by using a particular twist of your hips to create a high velocity spin on the football. The directional velocity of the spin will reduce the impact of air pressure differential that may impact the ball's ultimate trajectory." Although the message is the same, students might feel intimidated by the language and conclude that science is not something for them. Therefore, when we fail to respect the cultural diversity that people bring to conversations, we fail to understand the intelligence of those who have incredible ideas simply because they are using language that we do not associate with brilliance.

The affective aspect of the language-identity dilemma involves how we feel when we use particular words. For some, saying words like *mitochondrion* or *electrostatic forces* can make them feel like outsiders. Students have found themselves in situations where they sit in their chemistry or biology class and feel apprehensive as the teacher pours forth a stream of incomprehensible science terminology. In these moments, content is not the primary issue. The primary challenge involves how young people feel when science is taught in a language that is symbolically and culturally different from their own.

These interactions with the spoken and the written language of science make up the affective aspect of the language-identity dilemma; that is, the way we teach science without regard to how science language sounds can make people feel uncomfortable. The idea that language interactions include moments that send the message "You do not belong" is well researched in sociolinguistics. Agar describes these unique language moments as *rich points*, instances in conversations where the subtle cues of talk send you a message that you are not a member of the language culture of the people you are communicating with. These include instances when you do not get a joke because you lack an understanding of the cultural context that informs its humor. Rich points also include moments where the differences in word meanings send you a simple message: "I am from another culture."[2] In science, minority students often find themselves in situations where the complex language of the classroom sends them messages of cultural conflict. They may feel as though they are at a language disadvantage because the teachers ignore the language culture of the classroom.

The language-identity dilemma suggests that one of the problems in science teaching is not taking language seriously. If we do not take a careful stance on how language impacts learning, we can put students in a position where they cannot understand. As I've noted, science presents the unique challenge of teaching both new ideas and new concepts simultaneously. However, how much of our research and training focuses on how we will teach the language of science. This process can confuse students as new ideas are clouded by the new words used to represent them.

PROVING THE AFFECTIVE DOMAIN

The fundamental challenge in educational research is testing ideas. When scholars identify better ways to teach, they are not afforded opportunities to simply walk into a school and run an experiment to see if these new ways of teaching will work better. Imagine walking up to a principal and asking, "Can I teach one group of your students in a way that really works well and the other group of students in a way that doesn't work at all?" There is a natural conflict. Though researchers want to test innovations, schools understand just how precious every moment is with their students. The result is a field of research where people know a lot about how to teach but can't scale the research because they do not have experimental data to demonstrate how well it works.

In my research on how language impacts learning, I found myself in a complicated situation. On the one hand, I wanted to prove what I knew to be right. I myself have been in classrooms most of my life where people assumed I was not intelligent because of the way I spoke. As a teacher, I had numerous conversations with students about the language of science in their language or culture. I knew it was right. However, for the sake of research, I did not want to do what everyone else had already done. I could simply ask the students how they felt about being taught with complex language, but that did not feel like enough. I needed something more.

One of the benefits of being at a world-class institution is that you often come across world-class scholars. At the time, Stanford University professors were engaging in incredible experimental studies about students. I began to ask myself if I could borrow something from these brilliant psychologists. I did just that, reading about how scholars subtly intervened by introducing a seemingly unimportant cue to see if it impacted students' performance. One afternoon, I had the privilege to sit in on a lecture by the late Nalini Ambady.[3] Her work used a simple cueing strategy. In one study, she gathered a group of young girls and asked them to color coloring book pages with images of girls.[4] Another group colored pictures that were not gender-based. After they had finished, Ambady asked the girls to do a series of math problem. She found that the students who had colored pictures of girls performed worse than the students who had colored pictures that were not gender-based. Her conclusion was that suddenly sending signals of gender triggered an ingrained negative stereotype of themselves as girls that caused underperformance. The work was sad, though the findings were dramatic.

Where her research began to truly blow my mind was when she attempted to do the opposite: using stereotypes to *improve* students' performance. She did this using the cueing method again, this time with the goal of triggering positive stereotypes. The approach was the same. In the study, she asked girls to color pictures. One group received images of obviously Asian people, intended to cue the positive stereotype that Asian people are good at math. The others received neutral images that did not signal race, but signaled gender. This was intended to cue negative stereotypes about gender and math. Girls who were subtly sent messages about positive Asian stereotypes performed better than girls who were not sent that message. The truly amazing aspect of the outcome was the way that all the girls, regardless of their race, improved their performance when the positive stereotypes were cued.

I asked my psychologist friends how I might borrow some of the principles of cued research to explore how language produces an affective response. They advised me to create two conditions. In one, students should be taught using academic language. In the other, students should be taught with simple, everyday language. In other words, say the same thing, but say it differently. The question was, *How I could measure the biological impact on students?* I had spent the previous five years studying and learning outcomes. This time I was curious about the affective impact. Could the language of science negatively impact students by producing stress or anxiety? My colleagues suggested that I assess the students' learning by capturing their cortisol levels after teaching them. Cortisol is a hormone that is present in people's saliva when they are feeling stressed. This was a great idea, but I could not imagine any school allowing me to teach their students and then take a biological test of stress.

After careful consideration, we came up with an alternative. I learned that in psychology there are a number of tests designed to assess students' stress levels. These assessments do not actually measure stress; instead, they test how being placed under pressure limits a person's cognitive capacity. I was pointed towards two tests (see figure 5.1). The first was the Stroop test, which is a measure of cognitive capacity. The task is seemingly simple. You read a word that is written in a particular color. The word that is spelled out may not be written in the color of the word—the word *red*, for example, may be written in red or it may be written in blue. When the word appears on a screen, the subject uses a keyboard to type the first letter of the color that the word is written in. So, if the word *blue* is written in red, you would

FIGURE 5.1   Example of Stroop and Flanker tests

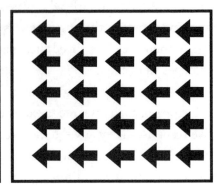

push the R button to recognize the color red. The challenge is maintaining enough mental focus to ignore what the word says and focus on the color that the word is written in.

The second test is a similar test known as the Flanker test. In this test, the individual must identify the direction of the centermost arrow. If all the arrows are pointing left and the center arrow is pointing left, you must click the button on the keyboard for the arrow that is pointing left. However, if the centermost arrow is pointed right while all of the other arrows are pointed left, you must click the arrow on the keyboard that is pointing right. This test operates in a similar fashion to the Stroop test. You have to ignore the majority of the arrows and identify the direction of the center arrow.

The goal of both the Flanker and Stroop tests is to identify when cognitive interference, like stress, prevents people from quickly performing the cognitive task. The question is not whether or not a person can accurately recognize a color or identify the direction of an arrow. These are easy tasks. The question is how long it takes. If you are under stress, it may take you longer to identify the pattern. So, if subjects are slow to recognize these patterns, we can assume that they are under some sort of stress or cognitive conflict.

Both the Flanker and Stroop rely on two types of items. Stroop congruent items are test items where the color matches the written word—the color and the word are the same. For congruent Flanker items, the center arrow and all other items are pointed the same direction. These are easy, because there is nothing to distract you. For congruent items, all of the information is headed in the same direction. Incongruent items are different. These are the items where students receive contradictory information. In the case of incongruent Stroop items, the color of the word and the word do not match. For example, the word *blue* would be written in red, thus sending incongruent information. In the case of the Flanker items, the center arrow faces the opposite direction of the other arrows. Where this becomes challenging is that it requires more cognitive work. You must ignore one set of information while focusing on the other.

Think of it this way. Have you ever found yourself having a great time while driving your car? The music is playing and you are enjoying the rhythm and the bass of your favorite song. Life is good! But when you go to parallel park, you decide that the best way to do it safely is to turn down the music. Turning down the music helps you focus by removing a distractor. In the case of our science language experiment, to accurately identify the answers on the Stroop and Flanker tests, people have to take more time. Taking more time is equivalent to turning down the music.

Our design was simple. We created two YouTube videos explaining the water cycle. Both used the exact same images and were the exact same length. The only difference was the words used to explain the cycle. Figure 5.2 illustrates the language differences used in the experiment. To make sure the conditions were equitable, we made the explanations the exact same word length. If the data revealed a consistent pattern on both types of tests, it was not due to error. A consistent pattern would prove that complex science language can cause affective differences for students.

FIGURE 5.2   The water cycle: Video screenshots from both conditions

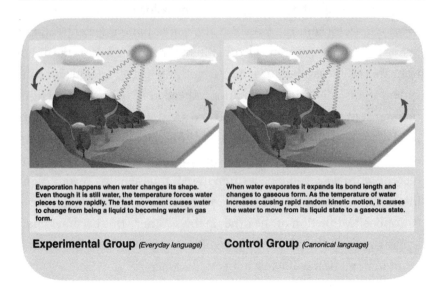

Evaporation happens when water changes its shape. Even though it is still water, the temperature forces water pieces to move rapidly. The fast movement causes water to change from being a liquid to becoming water in gas form.

When water evaporates it expands its bond length and changes to gaseous form. As the temperature of water increases causing rapid random kinetic motion, it causes the water to move from its liquid state to a gaseous state.

Experimental Group *(Everyday language)*   **Control Group** *(Canonical language)*

WHAT DID WE DISCOVER?

We brought a group of sixty-four students to campus. To reduce the possible impact of teacher skill, all students were taught by a brief instructional video. Students were randomly assigned to either the control (complex language) or treatment (simple language) condition. Figure 5.3 offers a representation of the experimental design. As the image highlights, both groups were taught about the water cycle and were immediately given the two stress measures; the Flanker Test and the Stroop Test. Both test measures how people perform under pressures that cause stress and cognitive challenges.

The findings affirmed our assumptions. Take a look at figure 5.4. In most experiments, intriguing experimental results would include the treatment group demonstrating a larger numerical result than the control group. Given that stressed students are expected to perform more, higher numbers mean greater amounts of cognitive conflict. In

FIGURE 5.3   Representation of the experimental design

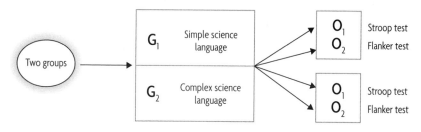

Note: O_1 = Outcome 1 Stroop test, O_2 = Outcome 2 Flanker test, G_1 = Experimental group, G_2 = Control group.

FIGURE 5.4   Results of students' reaction rates per test

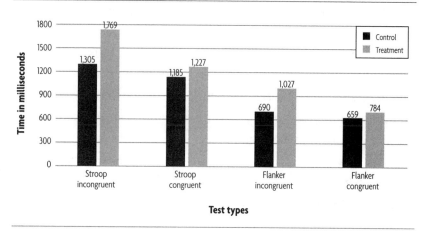

all of the conditions, the students who were taught using complex language were slower to recognize the patterns, thus the larger numbers. These results were statistically significant when those items were incongruent. Simply said, when the task became more complicated, the simpler language freed these students to think.

What could this mean? Could learning science through complex language leave students with a verbal disadvantage? The data was clear. There is something about teaching students with complex science language that produces a negative impact on students' capacity to focus. They can learn, but they have to turn the music down. What is clear from this study is that if we teach students without paying close attention to the language of instruction, we are creating an additional barrier. We are creating a verbal disadvantage.

IMPLICATIONS FOR TEACHING

Whether we think about the language of science as a verbal advantage or disadvantage, understanding how language impacts students has implications for teaching. Knowledge of language should change how we think about science curriculum. The videos and lectures used to introduce science ideas must take the language-identity dilemma into account. This knowledge of language should also alter the way teachers prepare students to learn the concepts and terminology associated with school. This has implications for teachers' training, pedagogical practices, and curricular development. Establishing a detailed understanding of language and learning can enhance contemporary teacher practice in meaningful ways.

One way teachers can use the knowledge gleaned from our research on the affective impact of science language is to make curricular modifications. How often do students in classrooms get an opportunity to explain what they know? More importantly, how often do teachers create opportunities for students to use their own discourse practices to explain an idea? Whether teachers create time for students to explain ideas in their own words or require students to practice using science language, they create new classroom norms. A curriculum informed by an understanding of language and its impact on science learning would focus on introducing ideas in simple, accessible language. To reduce the cultural and cognitive impact, learning should start with language that the students know.

As teachers create curriculum, they should ensure there is time for students to practice language. They should also make a distinction between *concept vocabulary* and *support vocabulary*. Studies on the communication of science suggest that students often struggle more with academic terms that are not the ones being taught in a given chapter.[5] This suggests that teachers must modify their curriculum to ensure they are teaching the language necessary for learning, and they should provide access to ideas by being careful with how language impacts students' understanding and connection to the discipline.

The language-identity dilemma is fundamentally about making sure every student has a verbal advantage by focusing on classroom discourse. Whether they are teaching spoken or written discourse, teachers should create learning environments where students understand that they are learning a new language. Thus, it is crucial to create activities that provide them an opportunity to explain ideas, practice using science language, and gain a metacognitive awareness of what they are trying to do. In the same way that Spanish teachers are comfortable asking students to use Spanish exclusively in the classroom to practice the new language, science teachers must take a similar approach. To make sure students learn, we must avoid teaching new ideas and new language simultaneously.

Another potential application for teaching involves a need to rethink how we train teachers. We often ask our science teachers to do too much. Unfortunately, we have an expectation that people will intuitively understand how to integrate the academic with the sociocultural. But why would a chemist or a recent physics graduate have a grasp of how language learning and culture implicate students of color? Teacher educators must provide extensive training to both future and in-service teachers so they can learn to view the world from a lens that is not binary. An answer cannot be seen as merely right or wrong. We need to be able to disaggregate what students know by taking a careful look at how the language they use represents their understanding. Chapter 6 is dedicated to exploring specific instructional practices associated with the language-identity dilemma and focuses on the ways that language can be used as a resource for helping students see themselves as part of the science community.

CROSSING THE BRIDGE

It was the wonders of a traffic jam that introduced me to Verbal Advantage. Thinking about the ridiculous claims that vocabulary equals intellectual superiority shed light for me on how the world thinks about language. Apparently, smart people use big words. If this is the case, then what does it mean when people choose not to use complicated terminology? I, for one, like people to understand what I am trying to communicate. As a result, I consciously choose words that people will understand and try to use the language of the culture I am in at the time. But the cultural bias is clear and sickening. When people refer to "high culture," they are often suggesting aspects of white culture. Hip-hop lyricism is not considered a high cultural art, and local cultural language is often seen as unintelligent. The challenge lies in preparing science teachers to value and understand the cultural benefits of all languages and dialects. If people wanted to sound like university professors, they would choose to use the language practices of university professors. What many simply do not understand is that people take great pride in sounding like their community. There is a true verbal advantage to hearing a voice, an accent, or a phrase that sounds like home. People gather around language in the same way they gather around a meal. It provides a place to connect, find common ground, and become a family. Language is liberating. It gives people the freedom to signal who they are to those they encounter, and it can truly provide an advantage to those who know the game. The next generation of effective science teachers must learn to provide a verbal advantage to a diverse and multilingual generation of students by integrating their home language with school science.

CHAPTER 6

The Hero Teacher

The Generativity Principle

SHE HAD CANCER. This woman, who would arrive to her class each morning with great energy, a warm smile, and loads of charisma, had cancer. In her wisdom, she chose to tell everyone, a strategy rooted in the deep love she held for her kindergarten class. Mrs. Jody, that hero teacher, let us know that she was fighting cancer and wanted the kids to be prepared for any changes that they would notice. If she changed her hair or lost weight, there would be no surprise. If there were to be a mural painted in her honor, as the school had done after losing another teacher to breast cancer the year before, there would be no surprises. Everyone knew.

Her openness created concern for some parents. Could a teacher fighting this battle teach their children? How would she teach as she dealt with chemotherapy and radiation treatments? Would she be around enough to offer the students a world-class education? In the end, the unstated concerns were nearly as awkward as the disturbing conversations. My wife and I noticed a troubling pattern. Parents would arrive to school and engage the hero teacher in discussions about cancer, asking her how her treatments were going. Those in the medical field would attempt to offer on-the-spot medical advice. I stood there and listened as they told stories about family members and relatives who lost their fights with cancer. What were they thinking? Although well-meaning, these conversations made me feel uneasy. I assumed that the hero teacher might find some solace in living in a children's world for a few hours, where her cancer did not matter.

One day, I attempted to distract her and beat the weirdo parents to the punch. I had noticed that all of my daughter's reading lessons involved a picture she had drawn herself. Not knowing if the practice was normal or something she had invented, I asked her about the process. She explained that she had adopted a three-stage approach to reading instruction. First, she would ask her kindergarteners to draw and color a picture. Second, after drawing the picture, she would ask them to write the story of the picture in pencil. Third, she would correct any misspelled words, write the correct spelling in pencil, and ask the children to correct the spelling. I thought this was fascinating. She knew and expected they would spell words incorrectly en route to learning how to spell.

When I asked why she taught reading this way, Mrs. Jody, in true hero fashion, offered this beautiful explanation. She told me that when the kids draw the pictures, it is *their* story. Because they wrote the story, they understood the context of the narrative. As a result, the text was simply a symbolic representation of the story that they already understood. She added she believed in *encoding.* In her view, encoding was the process of making symbolic representations of ideas you already knew. She argued that it was better than *decoding*, which was attempting to make sense of symbols that represent someone else's story. Needless to say, the hero teacher had done it again. She had saved the day. My mind was blown! Not only was I impressed at the strength it took to continue to teach under her circumstances, but I was also mesmerized by the depth of her under-standing and the intentionality of her practice and the new ideas I had learned that day.

ENCODING VERSUS DECODING

This short conversation sparked an intense curiosity about teaching and learning for me, and I struggled to find research that either con-firmed or refuted her wisdom. I wanted it to be right. It felt right. If students knew the context and had an opportunity to make sense of the representations, wouldn't they learn better? More importantly, I looked for science education research that explained if meaning-making was more efficient if instruction started with students' own interpretations. What I encountered were perspectives that orbited the hero teacher's wisdom but also affirmed her insight.

I found two complementary frameworks on learning connected loosely with the encoding framework. First, diSessa's work on p-prims suggests that students held intuitive understandings of phenom-ena that were useful precursors to rich scientific understandings.[1] The notion of accessing students' intuitive understandings has a long history in science education research. The insight that diSessa brings to the science education community is the idea that if we al-low students an opportunity to generate their own understanding, their intuitive descriptions of science ideas will hold profound sim-ilarities to the ones we intend to teach. In fact, diSessa argues that by accessing students' ideas first, teachers are better positioned to support them on their path toward understanding. From a teach-er's perspective, diSessa's work suggests that if we allowed students to develop their own understanding prior to attempting to explic-itly explain the idea, the students would learn better, in the same way that handing a student a basketball and telling them to shoot would allow them to get a feel for the process prior to receiving actual instruction.

Where the idea of p-prims finds synergy with the idea of encoding is the manner in which both assume that providing students access to the content prior to trying to "teach" it will give them a richer context for learning. From a teaching perspective, the idea is fairly simple: allowing students to articulate their ideas and providing them with several opportunities to explain a concept will help them build a foundation.

The hero teacher was onto something that extends the notion of p-prims. She believed that the process of writing and erasing was the act that generated understanding of spelling. Her idea of encoding assumed that it was better to separate decoding and contextual understanding. If the kids provided the context, they were better able to learn the symbols that represented those ideas.

What generates an understanding of a science concept? Many teachers will tell you that there is no greater resource for developing understanding than teaching something. When you have to teach, you engage in a twofold process. First, you question whether you understand something or not. Second, you determine the best approach of sharing that understanding. The question that haunted me when thinking about the hero teacher's encoding/decoding approach was, "How often do children have an opportunity to teach things as a means of learning them?" In most classrooms, we use explanations as our final assessment. But if explaining generates understanding, then shouldn't our classrooms be places where students get lots of opportunities to explain and help develop their understanding? As students are asked to explain things, the process of explaining will provide students an opportunity to build a clear understanding of the concept. That question led me to a second framework that supported the hero teacher's encoding approach to teaching: *the self-explanation effect.*

THE SELF-EXPLANATION EFFECT

The *self-explanation effect*—the idea that explaining things produces un-derstanding—reflects the essence of the decoding-encoding framework shared by the hero teacher. This idea, which emerged from contemporary learning science research, finds its roots in years of research studies conducted by Michelene Chi at Arizona State University. The premise is that the process of producing an explanation provides students with immense cognitive benefits.[2] Science teachers will often share the idea that the process of teaching helps them learn because it requires them to develop a much clearer understanding of the concepts.

Although teaching science and learning science content are fundamentally different, the process of self-explanation is vital to both. In a review study that offered a meta-analysis of years of study on self-explanation research, Fonseca and Chi explain: "Self-explaining is a learning strategy in which a learner elaborates upon the presented sentences or example lines by relating them to prior knowledge, making inferences from them, and integrating them with prior text sentences or example lines." The authors describe self-explanation as "learning strategy," highlighting how the process of producing an explanation requires students to integrate prior knowledge and make inferences.[3] The key subtext of their narrative involves the specific actions required to gain a cognitive benefit from the process of self-explanation. The idea that having students elaborate on ideas, relate science to prior knowledge, and make inferences suggests that effective teaching would provide students opportunities to engage in activities that mirror the learning activities described. From a theoretical perspective, the self-explanation effect is that learning occurs most efficiently when students have an opportunity to explain a science idea for themselves.

One of the unique aspects of the self-explanation effect is the depth of research available to support the idea. Though many educational theories describe learning perspectives and practices, these concepts are rarely supported by both qualitative and quantitative experimentation. The self-explanation effect is unique in the manner in which it has been thoroughly studied. In a recent handbook on multimedia learning, Fonseca and Chi outline a thirty-year pattern of research that proved time and again that those who were taught in a manner that required them to explain an idea remembered and retained the information better than those who were not given this challenge.[4] The assertion is quite powerful and supports the hero teacher's approach. If students are provided a chance to explain the ideas being taught, they will develop a deeper understanding of the meaning of the concept. As Fonseca and Chi note: "[Chi] observed students studying worked-out solution examples of physics problems and found that the most successful performers generated more self-explanations than the less successful performers. In addition, they found that the self-explanations from the successful students were more principle-based than those generated by the poorer performing students. Numerous studies in the domain of procedural learning have replicated the relation between the generation of self-explanations and enhanced learning outcomes."[5] Given Fonseca and Chi's findings, imagine the contemporary science classroom. Who gets an opportunity to explain the ideas in a science classroom? How many times have students taken a test and realized that they understood only an aspect of a science concept? In most instances, we could argue that the teacher is the person primarily involved in the act of explanation. We can then assume that the teacher is the one who is learning during that process. Following from Chi's research, we can assume that this would prohibit students from having an opportunity to learn the content. According to the encoding notion of the hero teacher and confirmed by the research of the self-explanation effect, unless multiple students are constantly engaged in the process of explaining, evaluating, and discussing, we can safely say that students are not learning efficiently.

Imagine a science classroom built on the assumption that self-explanations, embedded in the students' cultural context, produced scientific clarity. The goal of instruction would be to immerse students into discussions that require them to *talk* about the science that matters to them in ways that would eventually lead to a rich understanding. Instead of walking into a classroom and being asked to do what my colleague Dr. Jean Lythcott calls "guess what was in their teacher's head," students would be asked to apply their knowledge of the scientific value of their lived experiences. As opposed to having the teacher explain the benefits and process of osmosis, students might discuss how marinating food is an example of the wonders of osmosis. If we soak meat in a mixture of seasonings and water (a solution), then how does the meat eventually end up with seasoning on the inside? The key to this encoding framework is selecting contexts that students understand. Teaching about marinating meat will not suffice. Teaching about carne asada, oxtails, and other cultural foods that students are likely familiar with will help trigger the encoding process.

A major shift in this framework for teaching would involve seeing students as experts who share their collective understanding. As opposed to relying on the "star student" as the one who knows "the answer," an encoding approach to science teaching requires all students to share their collective knowledge. This requires a paradigm shift from individual excellence toward shared understanding. More importantly, this mode of instruction would focus on providing all students multiple opportunities to "talk" (written, spoken, or pictorial representation) about the phenomenon and move from initial explanations one would expect to be broad and full of errors to detailed, accurate explanations. Ultimately, science teaching rooted in providing students authentic context and multiple opportunities to explain ideas will help students understand the concepts more deeply. It would truly be the hero teacher's encoding approach to teaching.

This process runs counter to the culture in many urban schools. Some of these schools operate on the foundational belief that a quiet classroom is a well-managed classroom. Despite the fact that explanations can be generated by having students write, when a quiet classroom is the teacher's goal, it challenges students' attention spans. Science educator scholar Christopher Emdin spent years of research and professional development trying to convince teachers and scholars alike that the culture of students inherently lent itself toward creating environments rich in instructional rigor and cultural authenticity. Emdin argues that a modern science classroom must be imbued with the possibility for students to celebrate their culture and science simultaneously. He asserts that if teachers did not make these opportunities to bridge cultures explicit, students might mistakenly assume the culture of science and the culture of students of color were not synonymous.[6] Emdin also explains how bridging hip-hop culture and the students' culture helped foster deep connections between students and the culture of the classroom: "I argue in Edmin (2008) that these tools promote students' science agency by allowing them to feel like they have control over what they learn, facilitating the belief they have the power to assess the structure of the science classroom, and supporting their position as part of a collective that is responsible for the restoration of each other's science agency."[7] The argument supporting building cultural bridges between students and the science classroom has substantial backing.[8]

Considering this issue in the context of encoding offers a new insight. Providing students an opportunity to explain science in the context of their lives gives them access to improved science learning in their own world. The hero teacher argued that understanding context makes understanding content meaningful. So too does using students' own discourse practices work as a primary means of learning. These practices range from writing songs and freestyle rapping to creating memes and comics, among numerous other explanatory practices. The big idea, however, is that providing students with opportunities to discuss science as a means to learning the content offers two primary outcomes. First, taking an encoding approach benefits from the self-explanation effect. Students who explain will become students who learn. Second, using a dynamic set of cultural resources like cultural modes of discourse and culturally specific contexts will allow students to see the value of science in their lives.

After considering the hero teacher's perspective, I began to question how many in the field think about teaching science. For so many years, the focus of teacher training and professional development in science was narrowly aimed at changing what teachers do. I do not suggest that what teachers do is not significant. Rather, the hero teacher's lens on encoding leads me to question whether or not the teacher's actions generate learning opportunities. As a young science teacher, I foolishly played the role of "sage on the stage." I worked to entertain the students with humor and exciting experimental activities. I rarely stopped to ask the vital question of whether I was being an effective teacher. When applying the hero teacher's encoding framework to science teaching, I recognized the need to focus on putting students in multiple situations where learning is necessary. An effective science classroom is an environment where the nature of learning tasks generates learning.

THE GENERATIVITY PRINCIPLE

The goal of instructional design is to select activities that produce opportunities to generate learning. The *generativity principle* is the idea that the evaluation of effective science teaching lies in an assessment of whether classroom activities generate learning or not. Generative learning tasks are those that offer students an opportunity to discuss science content in context and provide them with opportunities to move toward a complete understanding of ideas. Let me offer an example. As I noted in chapter 3, for many years, I worked as a baseball coach. My job as a science teacher influenced me to coach by explaining physics principles. I spent a great deal of time describing how things worked and why particular techniques were important for my players to follow. Over the years, I realized that the best way to promote the players' improvement was to spend a lot of time sitting on buckets tossing balls to my players or hitting ground balls over and over again. One thing that coaches understand that science teachers do not is that a part of learning how to do things correctly is having extensive opportunities to fail. Doing things wrong and having an opportunity to correct mistakes through iteration produces an understanding of how to doing things correctly and proficiently.

In this way, the process of coaching lies in maintaining the balance between helping the players understand how things work and helping them practice their way toward mastery. When players understand what to do and have lots of opportunities to practice doing things right, we can assume they will quickly learn to do things the right way and understand *why* they must do it that way. Where coaches and science teachers are vastly different is in *where* they assume learning is generated. A coach assumes failure and practices generate learning. Many teachers assume offering detailed explanations to students produces understanding. The generativity principle sides with the coaches. In the same way that swinging and missing and then making a correction can produce understanding, the generativity principle assumes that answering a question incorrectly, having opportunities to share your reasoning with other students, and then looking up accurate information and hearing from friends will produce mastery. A failed explanation is the first step toward an accurate explanation.

The generativity principle thus suggests that learning science is an iterative process, and teachers must carefully craft opportunities for students to generate understanding. Instruction should be designed to allow students to iterate toward expertise. As teachers plan their lessons, students should have multiple opportunities to explain science ideas, evaluate their accuracy, and apply them to a meaningful context. It is at that point when students have engaged with ideas and struggled with options that the teacher's role as coach has its most profound value. This is the hero teacher's approach: it assumes that creating learning tasks that include failure and revisions will generate learning. The ultimate assumption in a generative approach to teaching is that thoughtful instruction should allow room for students to explore ideas and explain toward understanding. So, the question that naturally emerges is what types of activities generate understanding?

GENERATIVE TEACHING TASKS

Science teaching should provide students with activities that *generate* learning. As a student, you may have experienced a situation like this. You spent late nights in the agonizing process of preparing for a science test. Six cups of coffee and two Mountain Dews later, it was clear (at least in your mind) that you were prepared. However, as you read a question on the exam and racked your brain for the answer, you suddenly realized you didn't know the answer. You thought you knew. But, in that very moment of attempting to answer the question, you realized that you really only understood a few aspects of the concept. This is a painful experience, and it does not have to happen this way. Instead of the assessment revealing that you had only a partial understanding, answering a series of similar questions days prior to the exam would have helped you diagnose your knowledge earlier. If science educators want students to learn, the students must be actively involved in situations that force them to talk, write, and draw until they develop a full understanding of the concept.

Generative instruction assumes that talking about what you know improves understanding. What we talk about most often is what we know the most about. Ask a student about Snapchat, memes, or Instagram and be prepared for details. How often do students get the chance to describe science ideas? The relationship is simple. If students *talk* about science, they will *learn* science. If they talk about the science in their community, they are likely to learn more and revisit what they learned because it is an integral component of their lived realities. Therefore, excellent science teaching seeks to teach students about the science in their lives and provide them ample opportunities to talk about it. The practices below outline a series of teaching approaches rooted in an understanding of the generativity principle.

A TIME OF TELLING: GENERATIVE FORMATIVE ASSESSMENT

The first instructional practice is perhaps the simplest application of a generativity approach to teaching. All formative assessments are intended to *measure* how well students are doing. The basic assumption is that teachers provide students an assessment and the students' responses will indicate how well or how poorly they are learning the content. But what if the assessment forced the students to understand the idea? This paradigm shift is the foundation of *generative formative assessments*. Yes, they are formative assessments. However, their goal is not necessarily to help the teacher diagnose how well the students are doing, though they can do that too. The goal of a generative formative assessment is to create an opportunity for the students to explain the idea. In this process of explaining, students and teachers can expect two outcomes. Either the student will realize he does not understand the concept, or affirm that he clearly understands it. In either instance, a generative formative assessment adds an extra dimension to formative assessments. Formative assessments should do more than assess what students are learning. They should also produce learning.

In order to design generative formative assessments, questions should accomplish three things. First, they must be used as exercises.

Students arrive to classrooms deeply inculcated in the test-driven culture that defines contemporary schooling. A generative formative assessment must be used as a teaching tool. We expect wrong answers and we expect discussions about the assessments. Second, such assessments should give the students a chance to explain the answers. An environment in which every student has a chance to explain a concept is one where learning opportunities are available to everyone. Using this type of assessment should also give learners an opportunity to explain the concept in a context they are familiar with. Third, the assessment should give students a chance to practice using the science language. The classroom culture should focus on practice. The difference between "Explain how protein is made in cells" is vastly different than asking "Explain how protein is made in cells (in your answer use words like *protein*, *ribosome*, and *endoplasmic reticulum*)." A generative formative assessment is practice, not a test.

Let me offer an example of how this might work. If a teacher wanted to see if his students were grasping how osmosis works, he might ask "Describe how water moves in the process of osmosis." A typical expected answer is bound to include the stock phrase: "Osmosis is the process of moving water from areas of high concentration to areas of low concentration." What the question lacks is meaningful context and practice with academic language. A generative formative assessment version of the same question might ask "Explain how osmosis describes why marinade works when making carne asada (be sure to use words like *semipermeable membrane*, *random kinetic motion*, and *concentration gradient*)." This version of the questions requires the learner to practice the academic language and transfers the concept to something the teacher knows the student will encounter at home. If the culture of the classroom is one where students understand that they are not being measured but rather learning through self-explanation, one could expect this exercise to generate learning.

There are two simple alterations to any science question: add meaningful contexts and require the students to use the academic language. The pedagogy that follows is a different story.

A quick question on the whiteboard with a specific request to use the language is a start. If used as an instructional tool, a generative assessment approach builds a community of talk where students and teachers co-construct meaning in important contexts. To maximize generative formative assessments, teachers should ask their students to write a response or to share with a partner. In a classroom where the only answer valued is the "right" answer, the only people who are applying the self-explanation effect to their benefit are the teacher and the one or two students who feel like they have the "right" answer. By contrast, a generative approach is designed to give every student an opportunity to discuss the content. After the students write or speak their understanding, the teacher cannot offer explanations of the concepts being taught to students who had opportunities to make sense of it for themselves. Traditional formative assessments find their value in the way teachers assess students' knowledge and provide feedback, but a generative approach hopes for a different outcome: creating changes for students to talk about the science.

A generative approach to formative assessment can be informal, or it can be a formally structured assessment item. Take a look at figure 6.1. This could be seen as a typical assessment item used in science classroom. The question essentially challenges students to understand the microscopic image of a group of cells and apply their understanding of osmosis to the image. In this example, a student is required to select the correct principle about the concept of mitosis and make meaning of the cellular model. If one were to apply the modern approach to formative assessment, a teacher's quick review of the responses can reveal which students understand the concept of mitosis. A generative formative assessment approach is different. It asks for more. How can we use an altered version of this formative

FIGURE 6.1   Sample of generative formative assessment

Take a look at the picture of the cells below. Which of the answers below best represents accurate information about cells?

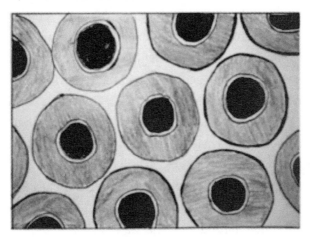

- Cells are different shapes because the DNA evolves.
- Each cell has identical genetic information.
- Cells are different shapes to maximize water use.
- Each cell has its own set of unique genetic information.

assessment to produce, or generate, learning? The answer to that question requires teachers to make two important alterations to the formative assessment questions. They must add context and allow students to practice using the new science language.

First, generative formative assessments are intended to produce meaningful science knowledge. This means learning more than how cells work. It could mean learning how cells work and how they impact daily life. An abstract question about cells is unlikely to be revisited in the students' home context. However, discussions of why people have dandruff, and having kids tell the story of how skin cells are able to replace themselves, is a context-driven way to teach mitosis. For a more culturally specific context, there are many communities where students discuss the problem of being *ashy*, a colloquial term for having dry skin. The story of mitosis can be taught by explaining how cellular duplication and a lack of moisture produce ashy skin. The point is to create a contextual situation that enables students to describe how and why mitosis matters. The hope is that every time they think about mitosis, they think about how it applies to dry skin.

The foundation of a generative assessment approach to science teaching is the idea that teachers should take time to allow their students to practice explaining science ideas. Generative formative assessments should be simple. Just ask your kids to talk about a science concept and use the new science terms. It is practice. If this practice is done in a context that matters in their lives, you are on to something powerful. The power of a question lies in more than just knowing the right answer. Using generative formative assessment will add something different: it will produce understanding.

SITUATING MEANINGFUL EXPLANATION: COGNITIVE APPRENTICESHIP TEACHING

A second approach to science teaching that will reap benefits for students is one that focuses on making sure students understand both the science ideas and the science language. *Disaggregate instruction* is a teaching approach intended to separate or "disaggregate" teaching the concept and language of science. As scientists made new discoveries, they identified the phenomena and then named them. The order of discovery and the order of teaching are different. In science, we teach new science ideas and new concepts simultaneously. In doing this we make learning science both confusing and intimidating as we hit students with a barrage of new ideas and terms.

Disaggregate instruction ensures teaching a science concept is separated into two parts. First, we want to ensure the students understand the big ideas. To do this, the teacher should offer explanations of key ideas without referencing new science terminology. Second, teachers must introduce the new academic terms. By splitting these components, teachers provide opportunities for students to gain a grasp of the fundamental concept and newly learned language of science in accessible ways.

There are four basic steps to disaggregate instruction lesson planning. First, the teacher must offer a pre-assessment. Second, the teacher must start instruction by introducing science ideas in simple, everyday language. Third, the teacher must introduce new academic language. Fourth, the teacher must provide multiple opportunities for students to use the new language. Together, the steps of a disaggregate instruction plan are designed to introduce students to the ideas and the language and support them in the process of talking toward understanding.

In the first aspect of disaggregate instruction, the pre-assessment is a valuable place to begin. As a teacher, you want to identify what context in students' lives will support their understanding of the concept. Additionally, you want to find out what language resources students use to describe the science ideas. As I recounted in chapter 4, I visited a local elementary school while I was studying process. At the start of teaching a lesson on photosynthesis, I asked the class a simple question: "How do plants grow, and what do trees need to grow large?" I was rewarded with a wonderful set of explanations of science ideas. Students said things like trees grow because they use "the bad air that humans breathe out." In another exchange, a student explained what they knew about the role about oxygen—that plants give us "the good air that we breathe in." Many also mentioned houseplants. These answers let me know what language resources the students used to describe photosynthesis and the context where they experienced photosynthesis (houseplants). This combination of phrases offered an everyday way to explain the chemical exchange that is key to photosynthesis. It provided a simple language to explain how plants release oxygen and how humans release carbon dioxide. Ultimately, understanding how to communicate with students provides a foundation to teach science in a way that is accessible to the students.

The second phase of the disaggregate instruction process is teaching the basics of the idea with simple language. To reduce the cognitive load placed on students, we start instruction by offering a simple explanation of the science ideas using accessible language. By reducing the language burden, the hope is that we are reducing any sense of anxiety and intimidation while ensuring students understand the concept. Imagine being offered an explanation of a science idea in a foreign language. For many students, this is what contemporary science teaching has become. By starting with simplified language, teachers can reduce the complication and help students develop a fundamental understanding of the idea.

The third component of the disaggregate instruction process involves teaching the science language. For many students, the first time they attempt to use science language is on a test. Teachers simply assume that this language is something students will acquire "naturally." However, if you ask those same teachers what the best way is to learn a foreign language, they would say to take lessons or go somewhere where there are lots of opportunities to use and practice that language. Where are students afforded the opportunity to speak broken science? Why do we fail to provide science students with those same opportunities? This second phase of disaggregate instruction begins this process. Only after the students understand the ideas that the terms represent should the teacher should plan to introduce the science terms. Once the terms are defined, it is important to explicitly ask students to practice using the new science terms. One way to do this is to use generative formative assessments. Ultimately, the key to disaggregate instruction is to understand that it is the teacher's job to provide opportunities for students to practice using science language.

The final phase of a disaggregate instruction approach to teaching is to scaffold multiple opportunities for students to use the new science language. The goal of this final phase is to transfer contexts. In a fashion similar to generative formative assessments, the final aspect of ensuring students have a masterful grasp of the concepts and the language is to allow them to use the concepts and language in multiple and unique contexts. Importantly, if students are explaining things they are familiar with, there is a greater likelihood that they will continue to use that valued information.

ENCODING AS A NEW PARADIGM

Returning to what I learned from the hero teacher, the value of encoding became increasingly clear to me. In her eyes, students develop a deeper understanding when they provide the context and she provides the practice. The decoding helped them to build spelling skills, but the narrative helped them to make sense of the science in their world. Her explanation of encoding versus decoding offered a fruitful analogy for me. If teaching is to impact students' lives, we need to make sure these students understand exactly how the science they are learning finds its meaning in their lives. By taking an encoding approach to teaching, we shift our focus from thinking of teachers as tellers toward thinking of them as people who put students in situations where they can apply their own context and practice their skills. Generative formative assessments and disaggregate instruction are two simple ways to take an encoding approach to teaching. However, the message is much bigger. The message is that impactful science teaching happens when we start in the lives of the children and empower them to make sense of the world in their own voice.

The simple conversation I had with the hero teacher left me changed. It opened my eyes. In the end, I have come to understand how to think about context, culture, language, and learning. But for her, the message is simpler. Heroes do what heroes do. They see the world, they make a change, and they empower others to do the same. At the end of the day, the hero teacher continued to teach and lead in the community. There were no murals erected in her honor. She beat cancer and lived to continue a hero's life.

CHAPTER 7

Strength & Weaknesses

Policy, Practice, and STEM Future

THIS FINAL STORY is one about a company you are familiar with. Although Netflix is now a household name, this was not always the case. In the early 2000s, Netflix took on the Goliath of the time: Blockbuster Home Video. Even the name *Blockbuster* indicated that it was a company that was difficult to reckon with. So, what happened to make Blockbuster a running joke and Netflix an American icon?

The story of Netflix has been a narrative that served as a teaching moment for me for the past few years. Reflecting on how it became the company it is today reveals an interesting pathway toward success. While Netflix was a young company, it found a way to *magnify its strengths* while simultaneously *fixing its weaknesses*. Although today many of us take for granted logging onto a computer, phone, or TV and being able to stream our favorite video or show, this was not always the case. Life in the 2000s was different.

In those days, a quiet Friday night at home could still include time for movie night. However, it was not what it is now. If you wanted to watch a movie at home, you would venture to the nearest Blockbuster

Video. You would find rows and rows of old and new movies—an expanse of shelves that stretched the length of the store contained every category of film. But, despite the vast selection, the offerings were far from perfect. If there was an intriguing new release that you had yet to see, you had to get there in time to get your hands on the last copy. If you were that unfortunate late soul who was unable to reach the store in time, you might find yourself holding an empty case, on the shelves only so that you could read the cover notes. Then you'd have to spend spending several more minutes roaming the aisles to find a suitable alternative. In some ways, the good old days of visiting the video store for a night of relaxation was anything but relaxing.

So, this is where the real fun began. If you were fortunate enough to beat the rush and rent that new hot movie, it might be a twenty-four-hour rental—you had to return the DVD or VHS tape the following day. If you failed to return the rented film, you would pay an additional fee. And if you were like me and often forgot to return your movies, a $3 rental might turn into a $50 purchase.

Netflix had an ingenious plan: it decided to operate as an online video rental store. To rent a movie, you would simply create a queue of all the films you would like to see, and they would send you the movies three at a time. All you needed to do was watch the films and return them by mail whenever you were finished. It was excellent! There were no additional fees, and you had a much higher chance of getting to see what you wanted. More importantly, you would not have to waste another minute of your life meandering through the thinly carpeted aisles of a dusty video store in order to find your Friday night entertainment. The joy of opening those packages and knowing there would not be any additional payment was incredible.

Oddly enough, the spectacular rise of Netflix did not lead to the immediate demise of Blockbuster. In fact, the very presence of Netflix in the early 2000s highlighted some of Blockbuster's strengths.

One major problem with Netflix was that you could not be spontaneous. If you wanted to watch a movie that night, you needed to plan at least three days ahead so the movie you wanted to see was in your possession. So, in some ways, both Netflix and Blockbuster had major limitations.

You may be asking what Blockbuster Video and Netflix have to do with science education. That answer lies in the way that Netflix carefully focused on sustaining its strengths while improving its weaknesses. During the same window of time, a company called YouTube figured out how to improve the way we watched videos. At that time, in order to watch a video online, you had to download the entire video and watch it after it was completely loaded onto your computer. This could take minutes or hours depending on the size of the video and the quality of your computer. YouTube figured out a way to send video in small components. Small pieces of the video would show up on your computer and disappear after you watched it. Thus, streaming was born. Netflix, now battling Blockbuster in the video rental business, was secretly following the lead of YouTube. It asked a question: "What if we could stream movies directly to our customers?" In this way, it could solve the "watch it now" challenge associated with renting films. So, while Blockbuster continued to master the art of being Blockbuster video rental, Netflix focused its entire advertising campaign on highlighting its strengths, using the simple refrain "No late fees."

In thinking about those early days of the business, I recognize that Netflix did not promise the moon. Instead of selling something that was not there, it focused on its strongest selling point. You all have been there. When people are trying to convince you to do something, they may speak with false enthusiasm. For example, in introducing you to the new vegetarian meat substitute, a friend might rave, "This incredimeat is so good, it's better than real beef!" If the friend has to sell it like that, it may not be so good. But, if your friend eats it all and can't wait to get more, the enthusiasm might be genuine. Similarly, if there is a line around the corner for the meatless hamburger joint, there is no need for overselling. You have something real. In the case of Netflix, it relied on its "no late fees" approach to marketing without making wild claims or promises, and could continue to develop improvements as they went along. In this way, Netflix was able to close the distance between itself and its Goliath by leading with its strength and actively correcting its weakness. We all know how the story ends.

The spirit of Netflix's endeavor was grounded in building a vision of the future that was rooted in the realities of today. The company knew what it was and worked diligently on building who they wanted to become. Science educators can learn something from Netflix (see table 7.1). A vision for the future of STEM education has to be rooted in understanding the contemporary state of STEM education while

TABLE 7.1 Science education strengths and weaknesses

Netflix			US Science Education		
Strengths	*Weaknesses*	*Work to do*	*Strengths*	*Weaknesses*	*Work to do*
No late fees	Required to wait days to access videos	Improve video inventory	World-class universities to train and provide teachers	Elementary school teachers, teaching to their weak suit	Improve pre-service and in-service relationships
Three guaranteed rentals	Limited access to some desired rentals	Reduce the need for DVD rentals	Wealth of knowledgeable scientists and science centers	Rarely teaching CS/Engineering directly	Rethink the afterschool 3:00pm to 6:00pm hour.
No need to leave home to rent	The user must plan their rental days ahead of time; there are no last-minute decisions	Solve "rent now" problem	Available scientists can benefit from working with K–12 educators	Assessment negatively incentivizes early science teaching	Invert the assessment process

planning for a future that is yet to exist. It is a vision of policy and practice that must highlight the strengths of the science education community while building on its weaknesses.

WEAKNESSES

When thinking critically about the contemporary state of science education, we can come up with a slew of weaknesses. In general, STEM educators have good intentions and are offering STEM education in ways never before imagined. However, the goal of this section is not to point out the failures of STEM education. The goal here is find ways to improve science education. As we think about how to do this, we must borrow from the wisdom of the Netflix narrative and build on our strong suits while thoughtfully addressing our limitations. I hope to identify the weaknesses in our current framework as a way to help us learn to address them. The first of these weaknesses involves the overreliance on large-scale STEM assessments to measure the goals of science education. The second is associated with the way we approach teacher training and teacher expertise. The third involves the current state of affairs in our curriculum development. The fourth limitation includes a critical need to recruit and retain diverse science teachers. Together, these fundamental issues threaten the way science education impacts our society.

Assessment . . . Weakness

One of the primary challenges with our current approach to science education is the manner in which assessment defines practice. Simply said, the tail wags the dog. While large-scale assessments enable educators to gauge our perceived progress, they also produce some dangerous side effects. As I visit elementary schools in the state of California, I notice a consistent pattern. Far too many teachers believe their sole priorities are math and literacy. When asked why science is an afterthought, teachers often share the same perspective. If science is not tested until the fifth grade, they know they are only measured by how well they teach English and math. Although the Common Core was intended to address this very real concern, it does not change reality. What incentive do elementary teachers have to teach science on a regular basis?

Imagine this in another context. If you were told that your job performance would be measured by your response to phone calls and face-to-face interactions with people, but five years from now it would be measured by how well you respond to emails, where would you spend your time? The most obvious impact is that you would prioritize phone calls and face-to-face interactions and would "try to find time" for emails. This is the current state of affairs in elementary science education. So ask yourself this question: If you were a third-grade teacher and your job and reputation relied on how well your students performed on their math and English assessments, how much time would you spend teaching science? Would you "try to find time" to teach it well? Although our culture as a whole is calling for improved science teaching and learning, our assessment priorities communicate the opposite.

This assessment-focused approach to STEM in the early grades carries over to middle school and high school. The need to prepare students for statewide assessments leads to a culture where covering a concept is far more important than ensuring students understand science ideas in depth. When you combine that with the fact that students are likely to experience a concept for the first time in middle or high school, the problem is magnified. Few people truly understand that our science standards are designed to teach a single concept at different levels of complexity at each grade level. Students should be introduced to basic categories in elementary school, should explore concepts in contrastive ways in middle school, and engage in deep analysis of application, prediction, and analysis during their high school years. However, the narrow focus on assessment has forced science out of our elementary instruction and created undue pressure on our middle and high school science teachers. The focus on statewide assessment is a true weakness of our current system and has served to undermine our K–12 science teaching.

Who Is Teaching Us: Science Teachers? . . . Weakness

The assessment challenge is compounded by the nature of the elementary teaching community. In many instances, elementary school teachers are individuals who did not major in scientific disciplines. As such, their memory of what constitutes science teaching is the high school chemistry, biology, and physics courses that they painfully, vividly remember. This association often leads to feeling intimidated by and uncomfortable with science. This ambivalence about science as a discipline hinders how effective and excited young elementary school teachers are about teaching it.

Many years ago, when school districts started hiring science specialists to teach science at every level of elementary school, this issue was thought to be solved. On a single day, an elementary science specialist would rotate through each K–5 classroom, teaching one lesson per period. However, as budget reductions framed school's priorities, these specialists were no longer viewed as necessary but were seen as luxuries. In their place, we saw the rise of literacy specialists who would visit classrooms to support emerging readers. Given the need to perform well on reading assessments, literacy specialists were deemed to be necessary, while science specialists were seen as accessories. The combination of the need to perform well on assessments effectively shaped the way we designed schools. The end result is that schools across America ask their elementary school teachers to be experts of every STEM discipline, despite their level of comfort. A STEM education for the future must carefully reconsider how we support STEM instruction at the elementary level by providing teachers and students the types of expertise and support they need to engage in high-quality science teaching.

A Curriculum for Everyone . . . Weakness

A third weakness in our current approach to science teaching is the way the current curricular products define what and how we teach. The Next Generation Science Standards were written to provide greater freedom for science teachers. They allowed for the professionalization of STEM teaching. Although the new standards are complicated, they are generic enough to allow teachers to teach what they want. Curriculum developers, on the other hand, have a different objective. The goal of curriculum developers is to sell more books. If they are to do this, the books must provide enough information to cover every state's standards. Simply stated, the more content in the curriculum, the easier it is to make the claim that the curriculum is aligned with state and national standards. Information sells. For curriculum developers, this variety allows the text to be broadly adopted. The negative consequence of this curriculum approach is that teachers use the curriculum as a teaching framework, mistakenly using the textbook as the curriculum guide and teaching chapter-by-chapter through the text. This deluges students with volumes of unnecessary information that is not rooted in their personal experience and expertise.

In the modern world, it has never been less important to remember facts. If you want to know something, you can google a question and the answer is at your fingertips. This is such a part of our culture that I can use the word *google* as a verb here and you understand exactly what I am referring to. Because of this, if concepts are to be understood and remembered, curricula must be rooted in the students' experiences. The best way for students to retain information is to encounter it in meaningful ways so the information remains relevant to their lives. Given the diversity of today's students, curricula must be flexible and adaptable so teachers can make it personal for them. Although interactive digital texts can be digitized and made customizable to include simulations, quizzes, videos, face-to-face discussions, and manipulatives, most of our modern textbooks are merely digital replicas of the same textbook designs we used in the early 1800s and 1900s. What should we do with contemporary curriculum? We will answer that question later, but it is truly a weakness that deserves a great deal of work.

The Teaching Force . . . Weakness

Another limitation of contemporary science education involves who teaches science. I want you to engage in a little exercise. Close your eyes and think about every chemistry teacher you have ever had in your life. While doing that, think about every physics teacher you have ever had in your life. What was the racial background of those teachers? Did they grow up in an urban environment, a rural environment, or a suburban environment? These questions are important for a few reasons. First, let me say that I believe teaching is a skill that can be learned. Regardless of the race and cultural background of the teacher, I am of the opinion that people who love children and know science can become excellent science teachers. However, teaching is a personal task. It is about getting young people to act on their own behalf and learn in the process of exploration. If all of the teachers are white, we will suffer from a lack of diversity in the perceptions held by teachers. A diverse teaching force has been demonstrated to have an impact on students of color. Understandably, the financial limitations of a career in teaching frighten some excellent scientific minds away from teaching, yet science is among the least diverse teaching fields in

America. However, this weakness must be explored as we reconsider how to build the science teaching force of the future.

To compound this issue, the teacher educators who are charged with the vital responsibility of preparing the next generation of science teachers share that same lack of diversity. Too many teacher educators have little understanding of the culture and multilingual identities of urban students, and they prepare teachers who share that same lack of understanding. As a result, what we get in schools, curriculum, and educational technology is an approach to teaching that fails to reflect the culture and interest of students of color.

Although the picture may seem bleak, the weaknesses in our current science education system are not impossible to correct. They are complicated and may take a great deal of time to examine, but they are challenges that can be addressed. We are in a moment that reflects science education's dichotomy. Although our field is rich with doubt and underachievement, it is also full of potential. There is hope.

STRENGTHS

Despite the gloomy image painted in the section above, science education is not without its strengths. I will address three of these below. One of its many positive assets is the simple fact that science fosters wonder and joy in children. Another strength of science is that when taught well, science can engage students in multimodal ways that other disciplines cannot match. A third strength—which may sound like a weakness—is that modern science education has set the bar so low that any new innovation is sure to have a revolutionary impact.

Wonder . . . Strength

Having spent many years as a science educator, I have seen firsthand that there is something fundamental to what we do that transcends race, socioeconomic status, class, and culture. Science amazes! My colleague Andy Gilbert describes science as a place where "wonder" never fails. Whether you are a five-year-old who is hungry after arriving at school, a seventeen-year-old committed to gang life, or a twelve-year-old curious about phenomena, when you are in a science classroom and experience something as phenomenal as an egg being sucked into a bottle by the power of air pressure, it never ceases to amaze. We have wonder on our side. It is the great equalizer. One of the joys of my year is hosting a science camp every summer. I have to tell you, eleven- and twelve-year-olds are not excited about attending a summer science camp. But the moment they experience air-pressure rockets flying three hundred feet in the air, they are captivated. In those moments, when they experience something truly interesting and realize they have been equipped to explain why it occurred, they are trapped by the power of wonder.

So, what does that mean for the future of science education? In my eyes, it means that we need to trust in the ability of science to grab our children's attention. The wonder of science is our "no late fees." Until we can improve the infrastructure and curricular design of STEM education, we can trust that providing students access to science will produce wonder and joy in their lives. Students love science when they can experience it. As I travel the country and visit science centers, aquariums, zoos, and science museums, I can enjoy the laughter and smiles as young people experience science firsthand. Conversely, I am shocked to see the lack of African American and Latinx faces in these science-centered spaces. As we move forward in preparing a new generation of scientists and engineers, we must work diligently to get all students involved in the culture of science at a young age. Simple visits to science centers and museums offer a start, but there must be a systematic focus on improving how we use wonder to integrate students into the community of science.

From a teaching perspective, this means moving away from tell-ing students about science and moving toward providing students chances to experience and explore science for themselves. We can rest our future on the fact that the wonder of science will never fail us. To be swept up in this wonder, kids have to get their hands dirty and ex-perience science phenomena regularly. These experiences will surely inspire children to pursue more because of the sheer wonder of sci-ence. It never fails to inspire.

Multimodal Learning . . . Strength

An underappreciated strength of science teaching is the fact that it can be multimodal. When taught well, science lessons can include opportunities to draw, build, talk, build models, conduct experi-ments, or watch videos. When they are in a science classroom with an effective teacher, students should be richly involved in a number of dynamic activities. If districts design curricula rich in multimodal activities, then teachers will be more likely to effectively engage in in-struction where students connect through the many types of activi-ties they have at their fingertips. In this way, one of the foundational strengths of teaching effective science is the mere fact that you can teach it in an interactive and engaging way.

Low Bar . . . Strength

This may sound controversial, but one of the inherent strengths of our current policy process is the fact that the standards for curricular effectiveness, school design, and STEM integration are low. Imagine a free online curriculum that is aligned with current standards. Such a product would be a life-changer for many teachers. It would enable teachers to save time on planning and to use curriculum they know is effective because it was designed by professionals. Today, teachers are sharing innovative practices and curriculum materials on social me-dia platforms like Pinterest. However, where are the science-specific sites that allow teachers to build a common resource of impactful science lessons? One of the subtle strengths of contemporary science education is the combination of the opportunity to build and the vast number of expert teachers available to collectively construct a database of highly effective science lessons.

The strength of science education is found in the nature of science itself and the need to draw on our vast intellectual and personal resources. As we think about policy changes and the potential to impact how kids experience the world around them, we do not need to look far. The engagement potential in the science itself offers a promising future. But the true potential of science involves its capacity to deliver materials to every teacher that can change how students experience science.

Envisioning a future of science education requires us to rethink what we do well and focus on the many resources we have available. Knowledge is different these days; we no longer need to retain information the way we used to. Our capacity to assign value to information is more important than ever. As such, teaching must rely on new ways to foster interactive learning. Additionally, our understanding of learning requires us to think carefully about how software can help produce learning. As we close this exploration of the intersection of race, language, culture, and science teaching, I would like to offer a few ways to innovate and improve science teaching and learning for all.

NEW INTERACTIVE LANGUAGE–CENTERED TEACHING

One of the most exciting new opportunities for science teaching involves our capacity to use technology to create engaging learning environments. In a stereotypical science classroom, teachers stand and lecture students about science concepts. Today, we can create learning environments where all students can simultaneously use simulations, watch videos, and engage in conversations about the content. Digital learning portals can truly transform teaching if teachers pair technology with best practices for science teaching.

One of the things that excites me most about STEM education is the possibility of software helping students understand the abstract content of science. Many people are fascinated by the interactive potential of software because it can be extremely engaging. I am less interested in what the software can do and more interested in how software enables teachers to provide learners with closer access to phenomena. The relationship between educational technology and school adoption is one that has been slow to mature. Schools do not adopt new technology quickly, and technology developers often fail to produce technology that is rooted in our best teaching and learning practices. Despite this distance, there is hope. One of the ways technology can help contemporary science education is by providing students with a sense of scale.

A common challenge of teaching science, chemistry in particular, is the fact that the phenomena studied can be so minuscule that they are difficult to conceptualize. In the past, if a teacher wanted to get a close-up of a phenomenon, the students had to use a microscope. If the teacher wanted to give students a macroscopic view of the world, they would use a telescope. It is not likely that teachers would have had a classroom set of telescopes. The fact that schools operate in daylight hours might also presents some challenges. If teachers wanted to take students places to experience phenomena, a costly field trip was the only option. This scale challenge associated with STEM teaching is an aspect where contemporary technology shines. It is time for schools to benefit from the *meso*, *micro*, and *macro* scale benefits of technology. I would like to focus on to two technology resources in particular: virtual reality and interactive digital textbooks.

VIRTUAL REALITY AND INTERACTIVE DIGITAL TEXTBOOKS: AN AUTHENTIC AND AFFIRMING SCIENCE EXPERIENCE

By using virtual reality software, students can experience *meso, micro,* and *macro* scientific phenomena at little or no cost. There is a general misperception that virtual reality software is expensive, but if students have smartphones, there is a great deal of potential. Cardboard VR boxes can be purchased for less than $5 a headset. For teachers who want their students to see cellular structures or give them a sense of subatomic structure, there are free VR simulations that will enable students to experience these phenomena for free. A simple YouTube search will also provide access to an enormous number of free VR resources. These resources provide innovative ways for students to experience science concepts. In real time, students can be embedded in the virtual world of a cell as a way to help them understand how things interact at the cellular level. Using VR, students may find themselves in a rainforest as a way to begin an analysis and discussion of ecosystems. The power of this new technology is that students can experience things at scales they could never have experienced them before. Because these resources are free, or at worst low-cost, they can also help reduce the resource gap between wealthy and impoverished urban school districts.

Using the technology alone is insufficient. The transformative power of new learning technology is found in the way teachers can help students engage in authentic learning experiences. If students are using software like Nearpod and Poll Everywhere we can now have all of them anonymously sharing what they think instead of having one person offer an explanation. Skilled teachers can use these opportunities to show students the way their classmates are beginning to think about the science ideas. They can also provide an opportunity for students to explore which of the potential explanations and ideas are most accurate. We have moved to the age of teaching science as argumentation. It is no longer sufficient for a student to simply explain how something works. A current approach will require students to explain why one explanation is accurate while challenging them to clearly articulate why other positions must therefore be inaccurate. This argumentative approach to teaching creates a scenario where all students have the opportunity to share their ideas and reflect on the ideas of others. Technology provides us this opportunity as teachers can put images on the students' phones, stream videos for students to watch, and allow students to discuss ways to interpret the phenomena. The students' answers can be shared anonymously for everyone to explore. More importantly, this process can provide a room full of teachers, as students switch fluidly between roles of explainer and evaluator. Taking on a language-focused approach will allow students to learn from their teachers and then be provided multiple opportunities to explain towards mastery and understanding.

The thing that I am most excited about in this new round of technology-based science education is the capacity to signal racial, gender, and cultural identity through learning technology. Think back to the science videos you experienced in school. Whose voice was used for the voiceover? Who were the scientists in these videos? Were they women? With the current flexibility of interactive digital textbooks, students can be embedded as the teachers in their own textbooks. Digital textbooks can include simple text, interactive maps, simulations, videos, text with additional information, and opportunities to write and share thoughts. And they can do this using diverse actors. Imagine if the faces and voices in the digital text matched the faces and voices of those reading them. Now, there is no need to imagine. In 2016, Kareem Edouard conducted a research study that focused on the impact of racial matching. The idea is that students can customize their interactive digital textbooks so the speaking voices, videos, faces, and images can all reflect their culture.

We are no longer in an age where the text must be static. Nor are we in an era where we have to wait for curriculum developers to offer texts that meet the needs of the community. In this new era of digital media, textbooks are flexible and have the potential to speak to the lives of young people. The potential of this approach is that we can now create digital textbooks that send messages that not only tell students they belong in science, but also allow students to be among those creating the science texts for the next generation.

So, what do digital textbooks mean for pedagogy? The implications are that using digital texts as pedagogy can make learning engaging and effective. As teachers consider ways to have students demonstrate their knowledge, they can have their students create short videos and texts. The video productions explaining key scientific phenomena can emerge as summative assessments. However, when students become coproducers of the content, the text can share an artistic and cultural flair. Imagine a group of young people in Oakland, California, who have the final assessment challenge of creating a video to explain protein synthesis. Students who speak with the love and brilliance of the East Oakland community could create learning videos that might be used to teach future generations from that same context. In creating these assessments, teachers are producing a wealth of instructional resources that can be dragged and dropped into digital science textbooks. So, as new students are being introduced to concepts like protein synthesis, they are being instructed by people who look like them. Apple offers an excellent textbook-creation software resource, iBooks Author. There are also other numerous comparable software resources on PC- and Android-based operating systems. All of these resources are free to download and use. Another resource could be CK-12, a nonprofit software company that provides free customizable textbooks that enable teachers to drag and drop existing content into place and add videos and audio to meet their needs. These days, anyone can use, build, and share customizable science curriculum. These materials can offer rich content and embed the literal voices of the science community.

The point here is to suggest that there is an inherent power in the use of technology. The technology we have available for us can enable us to see phenomena differently. A digital curriculum can do the powerful work of communicating who should be involved in science. As opposed to being passive recipients of a curriculum that does not speak to many urban students, technology-based alternatives provide content that reflects the community's interest.

EMBEDDING LANGUAGE

In returning to the language challenges described earlier in chapters 2 and 3, technology can provide an improved application of language-based science instruction. One of the fundamental limitations to a language-free approach to science teaching is that it does not allow students opportunities to practice using scientific language. With the new capacity of technology allowing students to engage with phones and iPads and share databases of answers, teachers can now create formative assessments that enable their students to explain science ideas. More importantly, instruction can provide students with a chance to share those ideas with their colleagues while practicing science language. The power of this process is that if teachers prompt students to become consumers rather than producers of content, they help students become science communicators who have a chance to use both their own language practices and science discourse as well.

STEM IS A NEW PRIORITY

Let's start with the obvious. I began my career as a science educator in 1996. At the time, I was studying to get my credential and master's degrees. People would ask me what I was studying, and when I would say "science education," the uniform response would be "What is that?" People simply did not understand what it was. When was the first time you heard the acronym STEM? We are in a new era where people have begun to take science education seriously. In the past, one of the primary rationales offered for improving science education was an assumption that a scientifically informed citizenship would lead to a nation of scientifically skilled individuals. The expectation was that an investment in producing scientists would yield fiscal results. After the recent recession of 2007, a US economy that was reliant on the stock market and banking had lost his way. The rapid regrowth of the technology and biotech sectors led many to double down on the bet that STEM was the key to financial prosperity. The end result is that we are now in an era where government, foundations, and school districts are deeply invested in improving STEM.

In the same way that Netflix skillfully sold us on the benefit of no late fees, we must trust that the current social and political support of STEM is useful in promoting STEM for all. The time is now for STEM educators to imagine, design, and implement transformative science and engineering programs. People want us to do a better job in teaching science mathematics and engineering, so we must use this strength to make a difference. The question is how.

To answer the question, I offer a pair of recommendations. The first is to teach science differently. As opposed to asking nonscientists to serve as our first teaching force, I would like educators to consider leveraging the power of the scientific community as a means of strengthening a modern science teaching force. Secondly, we must reconsider when and where we teach science. I suggest moving our focus away from a purely in-school approach to science and instead moving toward a model that integrates in-school and afterschool science programs. Together, these alterations have enormous potential for changing our current approach to science teaching and learning.

Convenient Outsider: Scientists

One of the things that makes science unique is the way it straddles the world of entertainment and education. There are museums dedicated to giving students opportunities to experience science firsthand. There are television channels with programming designed to help people understand how science matters to our world. The number of supplemental resources available for science teaching stands as a stark contrast to the resources available for disciplines like math and English. Have you ever been to a mathematics or English museum? Have you watched the writing channel or math network? That does not sound like fun to me. But one of the strengths of science is the wealth of scientists, science nonprofits, digital media, TV programming, and science museums that are committed to the common cause of providing rich science experiences to the young and old alike.

I am suggesting that a revolution in contemporary science education can occur by simply incorporating our greatest resource: the scientist. While middle and high school science instruction is led by people who have a wealth of scientific expertise, training, and education, elementary science teaching is different. It would be smart to embed more support at this critical juncture. We are asking people to be experts at multiple subjects and then we grow frustrated when they underperform in the teaching of science. If universities and researchers need to engage in outreach as a component of their work, then why do we lack deeper connections with science?

A second potential way for us to move forward is to stop working against ourselves. As described in the strengths analysis of contemporary elementary schools, we are asking people who are not experts at science to serve the primary role of introducing science to children. Often, their anxieties are transferred to our young people. How do we address this? One potential solution is to recognize that we have a wealth of scientists who would love a role in schools. How many of you have ever heard of daily afterschool engineering programs? Have you experienced an engineering program that operates from 3 p.m. to 5 p.m.? Have you ever seen a school's afterschool care program that focuses on teaching physics? I think you see where I am headed. If we have scientists and science centers that want to serve the community, then we should work to integrate them into elementary and middle school teaching in structured ways. Science centers, science museums, and scientists could offer schools supplemental teaching help that has the potential to offer robust support to schools. If we need to provide children with full afterschool programs, then why have we yet to allow our scientific communities to build empowering afterschool programs that enable students to learn science free from the shackles of assessments and standards? We have an opportunity to introduce students to the wonders of science by allowing them to experience it freely.

Capturing the 3–6

The second recommendation focuses on reconsidering what we think of as school science. There are extraordinary programs designed to provide students from all backgrounds access to STEM. These programs teach students coding, game building, engineering, and even biomedical sciences. However, they share the same design—bringing students into their facilities one day per month or providing enriching summer programs. While many of these programs are truly exceptional, their designs prevent them from having a daily impact on students. More importantly, if these programs do not have a home in schools, they will be made available only to parents who know what these programs have to offer. Given these problems, we must reconsider how the hours of 3 p.m. to 6 p.m. can reshape the way students have access to science. If schools were to offer science programs after school, they could provide immense support to what happens in school. It is among our simplest strengths and one that must be explored carefully.

WHAT'S NEXT?

There is a lot to learn from Netflix. In the same way that the company quietly addressed its weaknesses while proclaiming its strengths, STEM policy makers must mirror that process in education. As we make arguments about the perceived failure of STEM education, we may need to recalibrate our concerns. We often compare ourselves to small countries with dramatically different social structures. Our financial disparity, racial conflict, and multilingual population make us different. Our university STEM education remains among the best in the world, and we continue to produce a stream of elite future scientists. The problem is our lack of success with those students who are not considered elite. The next movement in science education's future must be to focus on educating its underserved. Changing the face of science education's future requires us to change the faces participating in science careers.

We do not need permission to innovate. In a world where innovation is valued, STEM leaders must adopt the bold approach that Blockbuster failed to. As educators, we cannot be afraid to innovate and challenge our current educational infrastructure. Many are surprised to find classrooms of 2019 are identical to classrooms from the 1960s. School districts and county offices have a powerful opportunity to work together to build something new. STEM education has wasted too much time allowing policy to emerge from state boards and university researchers instead of adopting a grassroots approach that flows from the teachers. Innovation is a necessity that has to happen through STEM educators at every level.

Finally, the future of STEM education relies on educators building better networks. There is too much brilliance and intellectual vitality in STEM educators across the nation to overlook. A new era in improving science education requires all interested constituencies to work together to build on our strengths while addressing our weaknesses.

Theory and Practice

EXCELLENT SCIENCE TEACHING must become a right for every student. One of the challenges of providing excellent science teaching for every student is the science education community's ability to train a generation of science teachers who understand the realities of our multilingual and multicultural society. What teachers must truly understand is where issues of culture intersect with the fundamental principles of learning. Effective science teaching practice, however, extends beyond understanding and stretches toward a deep connection between theory and practice. *Science in the City* attempts to offer a simple vision of how theory and practice matter in science teaching for urban students.

BIG IDEAS

If there is a single message that serves as the foundation for this book it is the idea that there is no cultural distance between students of color and a successful science education. For years, scholars claimed that there is an inherent conflict between the culture of a student of color and the culture of the science classroom.[1] One of the messages from *Science in the City* is that the culture of science is deeply rooted in the pageantry, beauty, and vibrant realities of the real lives of people of color. What successful teachers must be able to do is to provide the students with a vision of how the science we live through each day plays a vital role in our community. In fact, this vibrant community science is the same science we are learning about in our classroom. With that in mind, there are a few ideas I hope every reader can walk away with.

The Black Tax

The *black tax* refers to the additional hurdle or cost faced by many students of color for being a member of a science classroom. This is not to say that the language or the cultural background that people bring to a classroom is a deficit background. Instead, it is to say that as people arrive in science classrooms, they enter environments that bear the weight of the history, cultural expectations, and stereotypes about who can become a scientist. Students understand that if they do not speak in the way that the teacher speaks, the teacher might not see them as intelligent. This is the black tax. Students understand that if the clothes and hair they wear do not reflect what the teacher values, the teacher may be surprised by their intelligence. This chasm, where cultural and linguistic expectations do not meet, produces an added burden for students. This is the black tax. If we are to provide students with a high-quality science education, teachers must become fully aware of role the black tax plays in framing students' experiences. They must deeply examine their assumptions and biases to measure how they shape their views students. Once teachers fundamentally question their vision of who can be successful and what intelligence sounds like, they can then provide students with access to a world-class science education.

The Language-Identity Dilemma

The language-identity dilemma suggests that language stands as a central hurdle to the successful education of students of color. The dilemma is twofold. First, if students use language practices that do not reflect with what the teacher deems valuable, the teacher may not understand what students know about concepts. For the students, as teachers use complex science language to explain science ideas, students may simply misunderstand the content. Secondly, hearing and reading about science ideas in language that is overly complicated may send students a subtle message that they should not be a part of the science community. Given these challenges, the role of language can be seen as a gatekeeper to effective science teaching and learning. A vision for the science education of the future must include a teaching force that deeply understands how to include students' language practices as a valued part of the instructional process. It must also include explicit teaching of science language so students can become masters of the language of science. This language-identity dilemma is central to providing access to an increasingly multicultural and multilingual student population.

Encoding Versus Decoding: The Generativity Principle

The idea that science concepts are learned and solidified through self-explanation is one that has deep roots in the learning sciences literature.[2] Scholars have come to understand that those who have an opportunity to explain an idea regularly become the individuals who have a clear understanding of the concepts. The challenge in the contemporary classroom is who is the person most readily engaged in explaining science phenomenon? The teacher. So, it is no wonder that teaching science is one of the most effective ways to learn science concepts. But instead of allowing urban science classrooms to become environments where teachers focus on classroom order and quiet, teachers should know that if they want their students to understand an idea thoroughly they will need to provide them with multiple opportunities to explain the concepts. This idea—the *generativity principle*—is the foundation of effective science teaching. This will require a shift in expectation. Teachers can no longer expect students to be able to offer a correct answer and rich arguments on the first try. Instead, effective science teaching would allow students to engage in multiple explanations with an assumption that if they continue to explain and revise their ideas, they will talk (and *write)* their way toward fluency and scientific accuracy. The generativity principal assumes that teachers begin instruction with the expectation that they will provide their students multiple opportunities to explain the ideas prior to assessing what they know. In this way, formative assessment can both measure how students are doing and *generate* learning opportunities for science students.

EFFECTIVE PRACTICES

Science in the City was not designed to push teachers' understanding of theory. Instead, the goal was to provide a theoretical foundation for instructional practices that have been thoroughly tested. If we understand how valuable language is to allowing students to feel like a part of the classroom and we understand how important language is for their learning, we must engage in instruction that is built on these principles. In the same fashion if we understand how a shift in our framework for assessment might matter, we need to think about alternative versions of assessing science students so they can maximize their learning. As such, this book focuses on introducing teachers to a small number of instructional practices that are supported by the theories described above.

Disaggregate Instruction

Disaggregate instruction is the idea that effective science teaching must begin by reducing the language barrier as a fundamental gatekeeper to students' understanding. To do this, the teachers of tomorrow must begin instruction by introducing students to the big ideas of a concept in the most accessible language possible, considering how to remove and replace complex science terms with accessible everyday alternatives. If we offer students an explanation of a concept in simple language it reduces the barrier of their understanding. Students are now in a position to use their new science language to understand the ideas that they already understand. That instructional introduction can now be followed by the explicit teaching of the new science words. This practice is one that has proven to be effective and enhances learning for all students.

Generative Formative Assessment

Science education must rethink formative assessment. Formative assessment, which is now the norm, is known as an assessment *for* learning.[3] Most teachers think of formative assessment as a process where teachers determine what students have learned by asking them questions and then correcting their course of instruction to meet the needs of the students. *Science in the City* is pushing science teachers to reconsider this process. I certainly agree that formative assessment is *for* learning, but it can be re-envisioned. This new vision suggests that we use *generative formative assessment* as a way to produce or *generate learning*. That is, if we provide students with multiple assessment opportunities and allow them to correct these explanations through iteration, students will engage in a more efficient pathway towards learning. This is specifically impactful if these assessments ask students to explain ideas and ask them to use science language in these explanations. This approach will produce a deeper understanding of concepts and a mastery of the newly learned science language.

Culturally Based Cognitive Apprenticeship Instruction

Cognitive apprenticeship instruction is a teaching practice that has now been widely adopted throughout education.[4] The idea is to create an apprenticeship experience throughout the lesson plan, where teachers play a significant role in the beginning of the lessons and slowly move to the background as their students explain, make arguments, and build an enhanced understanding of the concepts. The stages of cognitive approach of lesson planning include establishing a problem, modeling in activities that are teacher-centered, coaching during student-centered activities, and finally fading away and providing students opportunities for assessment. As a lesson-planning approach, I argue that cognitive apprenticeship can be integrated with culturally relevant pedagogy.[5] For example, the first stage of a cognitive apprenticeship lesson plan is to establish a problem. This problem is intended to produce a necessity to learn the concepts. By using a culturally relevant issue, the teacher creates a situation that enables students to see the value the concepts in their lives, while leveraging an efficient approach to promoting students' learning.

Technology as a Cultural Mediator

A final pedagogical recommendation made by *Science in the City* involves a rethinking of how technology plays a role in teaching and learning. While I certainly agree that technology plays a vital role in helping students envision the multidimensional movements of science phenomena, there is so much more we have yet to examine. I argue that using technology in culturally specific ways can serve to build a bridge between the culture of the teachers and the culture of the students they serve. The videos, VR simulations, and digital textbooks that we now have available can reflect the culture of the students they serve. As teachers think about using technology, I would urge every teacher to find technological resources that use faces that are similar to those of the students you are teaching, that bear the sounds of the culture of the students, and show images of the culture students live in. In this way, technology has a unique potential to play the role of a bridge across cultures.

At the end of the day, this book reflects the many years of my professional experience and research. Children have the incredible capacity to learn anything we put in from of them. As we move forward in a new generation of science teaching and learning, I hope these lessons learned can serve students in urban communities across the nation. There is so much more we can do; we simply need to learn to bridge theory to practice in meaningful ways.

ADDITIONAL RESOURCES

Abraham, Reem Rachel, Faith Alele, Ullas Kamath, Annamma Kurien, Kiranmai S. Rai, Indira Bairy, Mohandas K. G. Rao, et al. "Assessment for Learning: A Needs Analysis Study Using Formative Assessment to Evaluate the Need for Curriculum Reform in Basic Sciences." *Advances in Physiology Education* 42, no. 3 (September 2018): 482–86.

Baugh, John. "Linguistic Profiling," in *Black Linguistics: Language, Society, and Politics in Africa and the Americas*, ed. Arnetha F. Ball et al. (Routledge, 2003), 155–168.

———. "Isn't That Just Good Teaching? Disaggregate Instruction and the Language Identity Dilemma." *Journal of Science Teacher Education* 22, no. 8 (December 1, 2011): 679–704.

Finson, Kevin D., John B. Beaver, and Bonnie L. Cramond. "Development and Field Test of a Checklist for the Draw-A-Scientist Test." *School Science and Mathematics* 95, no. 4 (1995): 195–205.

Gonzalez, Norma, Luis C. Moll, Martha Floyd Tenery, Anna Rivera, Patricia Rendon, Raquel Gonzales, and Cathy Amanti. "Funds of Knowledge for Teaching in Latino Households." *Urban Education* 29, no. 4 (1995): 443–470.

NOTES

INTRODUCTION

1. Derrick A. Bell Jr., "*Brown v. Board of Education* and the Interest-Convergence Dilemma," *Harvard Law Review* 93, no. 3 (January 1980): 518–533, https://www.jstor.org/stable/1340546?seq=1#metadata_info_tab_contents.

2. Valerie Purdie-Vaughns et al., "Social Identity Contingencies: How Diversity Cues Signal Threat or Safety for African Americans in Mainstream Institutions," *Journal of Personality and Social Psychology* 94, no. 4 (2008): 615.

3. David Wade Chambers, "Stereotypic Images of the Scientist: The Draw-A-Scientist Test," *Science Education* 67, no. 2 (1983): 255–265; Kevin D. Finson, John B. Beaver, and Bonnie L. Cramond, "Development and Field Test of a Checklist for the Draw-A-Scientist Test," *School Science and Mathematics* 95, no. 4 (1995): 195–205.

4. Purdie-Vaughns et al., "Social Identity Contingencies."

5. Purdie-Vaughns et al., "Social Identity Contingencies."

6. Luis C. Moll et al., "Funds of Knowledge for Teaching: Using a Qualitative Approach to Connect Homes and Classrooms," *Theory into Practice* 31, no. 2 (March 1, 1992): 132–141, Norma Gonzalez and Luis C. Moll (Mahwah, NJ: Lawrence Erlbaum Associates, 2005), 71–87.

7. Beth Warren and Ann S. Rosebery, "Equity in the Future Tense: Redefining Relationships Among Teachers, Students, and Science in Linguistic Minority Classrooms," in *New Directions for Equity in Mathematics Education,* ed. Walter Secada, Elizabeth Fennema, and Lisa Adajian (New York: Cambridge Press1995), 298–328; Ann S. Rosebery, Beth

Warren, and Faith R. Conant, "Appropriating Scientific Discourse: Findings from Language Minority Classrooms," *Journal of the Learning Sciences* 2, no. 1 (1992): 61–94.

CHAPTER 1

1. James T. Minor, "A Contemporary Perspective on the Role of Public HBCUs: Perspicacity from Mississippi," *Journal of Negro Education* (2008): 323–335; Russell H. Barrett, *Integration at Ole Miss* (Chicago: Quadrangle Books, 1965).

2. James D. Anderson, "Race in American Higher Education," in *The Racial Crisis in American Higher Education: Continuing Challenges for the Twenty-First Century*, ed. William A. Smith, Philip G. Altbach, and Kofi Lomotey (Albany: State University of New York, 2002), 3–22.

3. Catherine Prendergast, "The Economy of Literacy: How the Supreme Court Stalled the Civil Rights Movement," *Harvard Educational Review* 72, no. 2 (July 2002): 206–230.

4. Joshua Fishman, "Language, Ethnicity, and Racism," in *Lanuage and Ethnicity in Minority Sociolinguistic Perspective* (Philadelphia: Multilingual Matters, Ltd., 1989), 9–22.

5. Mikhail M. Bakhtin, *The Dialogic Imagination: Four Essays*, ed. M. Holquist, trans. C. Emerson and M. Holquist (Austin: University of Texas Press, 1981), 294.

6. Rosina Lippi-Green, *English with an Accent: Language, Ideology, and Discrimination in the United States* (New York: Routledge Press, 2004), 165.

7. Dorothy K. Williamson-Ige, "Approaches to Black Language Studies: A Cultural Critique," *Journal of Black Studies* 15, no. 1 (1984): 17–29.

8. Na'ilah Nasir, *Racialized Identities* (Stanford, CA: Stanford University Press, 2012).

9. John Baugh, "Linguistic Profiling," in *Black Linguistics: Language, Society, and Politics in Africa and the Americas*, ed. Arnetha F. Ball et al. (New York: Routledge, 2003), 155–168; Bob Blauner, "Talking Past Each Other: Black and White Languages of Race," *The American Prospect* 10 (1992): 55–64.

10. Williamson-Ige, "Approaches to Black Language Studies."

11. Fishman, "Language, Ethnicity, and Racism," 16.

12. Malcolm Gladwell, *Blink: The Power of Thinking Without Thinking* (Boston: Little, Brown, 2007), 86.

13. Gladwell, *Blink*.

14. Gladwell, *Blink*, 97.

CHAPTER 2

1. Dell Hymes, "On Communicative Competence," *Sociolinguistics* (1972): 269–293; Dell Hymes, "Models of the Interaction of Language and Social Life: Toward a Descriptive Theory," *Intercultural Discourse and Communication: The Essential Readings* (2005): 4–16.

2. Emanuel A. Schegloff, Gail Jefferson, and Harvey Sacks, "The Preference for Self-Correction in the Organization of Repair in Conversation," *Language* 53, no. 2 (1977): 361–382.

3. Hugh Mehan et al., *Constructing School Success: The Consequences of Untracking Low Achieving Students* (Cambridge, UK: Cambridge University Press, 1996).

4. Hansun Zhang Waring, "Moving out of IRF (Initiation-Response-Feedback): A Single Case Analysis," *Language Learning* 59, no. 4 (December 1, 2009): 796–824.

5. John Hughes, dir., *Ferris Bueller's Day Off*, Paramount Pictures, 1986.

6. Jay Lemke, Talking Science: Language, Learning, and Values (Westport, CT: Ablex Publishing, 1990), 35.

7. Jerry Wellington and Jonathan Osborne, *Language and Literacy in Science Education* (London: McGraw-Hill Education (UK), 2001), 65.

8. Rosi Lippi-Green, *"English with an Accent: Language, Ideology, and Discrimination in the United States* (New York: Routledge Press, 2012).

CHAPTER 3

1. Dedre Gentner, "Why Nouns Are Learned Before Verbs: Linguistic Relativity vs. Natural Partitioning," in *Languge Development*, vol. 2, *Language Thought and Culture*, ed. S. Kuczaj (Hillsdale, NJ: Lawrence Erlbaum, 1982); Dedre Gentner and Susan Goldin-Meadow, *Language in Mind: Advances in the Study of Language and Thought* (Cambridge, MA: MIT Press, 2003); John J. Gumperz, "The Linguistic and Cultural Relativity of Conversational Inference," in *Rethinking Linguistic Relativity*,

ed. J. Gumperz and S. Levinson (Cambridge: Cambridge University Press, 1996), 374–406.

2. Eve Clarke, "Languages and Representations," in *Language in Mind*, 17–24.

3. Lera Boroditsky, "Linguistic Relativity," *Encyclopedia of Cognitive Science* (Wiley Online Library, 2006), https://doi.org/10.1002/0470018860 .s00567.

4. B. A. Brown, "Isn't That Just Good Teaching? Disaggregate Instruction and the Language Identity Dilemma," *Journal of Science Teacher Education* 22, no. 8 (2011): 679–704, doi:10.1007/s10972-011-9256-x.

5. Ajay Sharma and Charles Anderson, "Transforming Scientists' Science into School Science," paper delivered at the National Association for Research in Science Teaching, Philadelphia, March 23, 2003.

6. Luis Moll et al., "Funds of Knowledge for Teaching: Using a Qualitative Approach to Connect Homes and Classrooms," in *Funds of Knowledge: Theorizing Practices in Households, Communities, and Classrooms*, ed. Norma González, Luis Moll, and Cathy Amanti (Mahwah, NJ: Lawrence Erlbaum, 2005), 71–87.

CHAPTER 4

1. Lera Boroditsky, "Linguistic Relativity," *Encyclopedia of Cognitive Science* (Wiley Online Library, 2006), https://doi.org/10.1002/0470018860 .s00567.

2. John Seely Brown, Allan Collins, and Paul Duguid, "Situated Cognition and the Culture of Learning," *Educational Researcher* 18, no. 1 (1989): 32–42; Jeong-Im Choi and Michael Hannafin, "Situated Cognition and Learning Environments: Roles, Structures, and Implications for Design," *Educational Technology Research and Development* 43, no. 2 (1995): 53–69.

3. Brown, Collins, and Duguid, "Situated Cognition."

4. Brown, Collins, and Duguid, "Situated Cognition."

5. Michael Pressley and Christine McCormick, *Cognition, Teaching, and Assessment* (New York: HarperCollins College Publishers, 1995), 179.

6. Lev Semenovich Vygotsky, *Language and Thought*, (Ontario, Canada: Massachusetts Institute of Technology Press, 1962), 281.

7. Bryan A. Brown, "Discursive Identity: Assimilation into the Culture of Science and Its Implications for Minority Students," *Journal of Research in Science Teaching* 41, no. 8 (2004): 810–834.

8. Full research articles available at: Bryan A. Brown, and Kihyun Ryoo, "Teaching Science as a Language: A 'Content-First' Approach to Science Teaching," *Journal of Research in Science Teaching* 45, no. 5 (2008): 529–553; Bryan A. Brown et al., "Pathway Towards Fluency: Using 'Disaggregate Instruction' to Promote Science Literacy," *International Journal of Science Education* 32, no. 11 (2010): 1465–1493.

CHAPTER 5

1. http://verbaladvantage.com.

2. Michael Agar, *Language Shock: Understanding the Culture of Conversation* (New York: William Morrow & Company, 1994).

3. Nalini Ambady et al., "Stereotype Susceptibility in Children: Effects of Identity Activation on Quantitative Performance," *Psychological Science* 12, no. 5 (2001): 385–390.

4. Margaret Shih, Todd L. Pittinsky, and Nalini Ambady, "Stereotype Susceptibility: Identity Salience and Shifts in Quantitative Performance," *Psychological Science* 10, no. 1 (January 1999): 80–83.

5. See, for example Jerry Wellington and Jonathan Osborne, *Language And Literacy In Science Education* (London: McGraw-Hill Education [UK], 2001).

CHAPTER 6

1. Andrea A. diSessa and Bruce L. Sherin, "What Changes in Conceptual Change?" *International Journal of Science Education* 20, no. 10 (1998): 1155–1191; Andrea A. diSessa, "Why 'Conceptual Ecology' Is a Good Idea," in *Reconsidering Conceptual Change: Issues in Theory and Practice*, ed. Margarita Limón and Lucia Mason (Springer, 2002), 28–60.

2. Michelene T-H. Chi, et al., "Eliciting Self-Explanations Improves Understanding." *Cognitive Science* 18, no. 3 (1994): 439–477.

3. Brenda Fonseca and Michelle Chi, "Instruction Based on Self-Explanation," in *Handbook of Research on Learning and Instruction*, ed. Richard Mayer and Patricia Alexander (New York: Routledge, 2011), 396.

4. Fonseca and Chi, "Instruction Based on Self-Explanation."

5. Fonseca and Chi, "Instruction Based on Self-Explanation," 297.

6. Christopher Emdin, "Affiliation and Alienation: Hip-Hop, Rap, and Urban Science Education," *Journal of Curriculum Studies* 42, no. 1 (February 2010): 1–25; Christopher Emdin, "Dimensions of Communication in Urban Science Education: Interactions and Transactions," *Science Education* 95, no. 1 (January 2011): 1–20; Christopher Emdin, "Urban Science Classrooms and New Possibilities: On Intersubjectivity and Grammar in the Third Space," *Cultural Studies of Science Education* 4, no. 1 (November 2008): 200, 62–65.

7. Christopher Emdin, "Urban Science Classrooms and New Possibilities: On Intersubjectivity and Grammar in the Third Space." *Cultural Studies of Science Education* 4, no. 1 (November 4, 2008): 239–254, https://doi.org/10.1007/s11422-008-9162-5.

8. Alberto Rodriguez, & Chad Berryman, "Using Sociotransformative Constructivism to Teach for Understanding in Diverse Classrooms: A Beginning Teacher's Journey." *American Education Research Journal* (2002), 39, 1017-1045.

CONCLUSION

1. Ohkee Lee and Cory Buxton, "Engaging Culturally and Linguistically Diverse Students in Learning Science," *Theory into Practice* 50, no. 4 (2011): 277–284.

2. Michelene Chi et al., "Eliciting Self-Explanations Improves Understanding," *Cognitive Science* 18, no. 3 (1994): 439–477.

3. Paul Black and Dylan Wiliam, "Inside the Black Box: Raising Standards Through Classroom Assessment," *Phi Delta Kappan* 92, no. 1 (September 2010): 81–90; Reem Rachel Abraham et al., "Assessment for Learning: A Needs Analysis Study Using Formative Assessment to Evaluate the Need for Curriculum Reform in Basic Sciences," *Advances in Physiology Education* 42, no. 3 (September 2018): 482–486.

4. Allan Collins et al., "Cognitive Apprenticeship: Teaching the Craft of Reading, Writing, and Mathematics," Technical Report No. 403, National Institute of Education, 1987, https://files.eric.ed.gov/fulltext/ED284181.pdf; Allan Collins, John Seely Brown, and Susan E.

Newman, "Cognitive Apprenticeship: Teaching the Crafts of Reading, Writing, and Mathematics," *Knowing, Learning, and Instruction: Essays in Honor of Robert Glaser* 18 (1989): 32–42.

5. Carol D. Lee, "A Culturally Based Cognitive Apprenticeship: Teaching African American High School Students Skills in Literary Interpretation," *Reading Research Quarterly* 30, no. 4 (1995): 608–630.

Teacher, researcher, community servant, and scholar **Bryan A. Brown** is the author of *Science in the City* and over thirty published research articles. A native of Oakland, California, Dr. Brown made a career exploring ways to improve science teaching for students in urban schools. In 2009, his coauthored research on disaggregating science instruction earned him the NARST award for outstanding research of the year. He also received the 2007 NARST award for outstanding early career scholarship in science education. Dr. Brown was also named a National Academy of Education and Spencer Foundation Fellow for 2005.

Dr. Brown's research explores how urban science education has underserved minority students by its failure to design instruction that is sensitive to the language and cultural needs of students of color. His early research projects led to the development of disaggregate teaching, an instructional approach that is designed to improve learning for underserved populations. He continued that research by examining how the language and technology can be used to improve science teaching for all students. Currently, Dr. Brown leads the Science in The City Research Group, which examines how technology can serve as a mediator between a monolingual and monocultural teaching force and the multilingual and multicultural student population.

INDEX